Leaving Belfort

Woody
Eugene R Widrick

The Memoir of Eugene R. "Woody" Widrick

Edited by

Nancy Shohet West

CONTENTS

~1~

The Place of My Dreams

My heart's in the Highlands, my heart is not here,
My heart's in the Highlands a-chasing the deer –
—   Robert Burns

Belfort, New York, is the place of my dreams. I was born there in 1932, left at the age of seven, returned for three years at the age of sixteen and moved away in 1951. I've made occasional visits back. In German, I read somewhere, there is the word *Heimweh,* meaning "homesickness," or "home-ache," but more than that, it is nostalgia and the pain of knowing that we cannot go home – as in Thomas Wolfe's title, *You Can't Go Home Again.*

When I do return, I find that most of the people I knew are gone, some of them I don't know where. One of my friends, rumour had it, a bachelor to the end of his life, had a pack of dogs and lived in squalor in a shack. It was so filthy that after they found him dead, all of his dogs were shot; and the shack, condemned by the health department, was burned by the volunteer fire department.

"Sorry about Wilbur," I said to my sister as we drove down the road he had lived on.

"Oh," she said, "He did all right. Built a nice house – there, that one – and was pretty healthy up to the end."

"What about all the dogs they had to shoot?" I asked.

"What dogs?" she replied.

It was a nice house. So much for rumour.

Wilbur's parents ran Lambert's Country Store in Belfort, New York. The Belfort of my memory, located about six miles outside of the Adirondack State Park, consisted of a district school, the Nortz House (later the Belfort Inn), St. Vincent de Paul Catholic Church, a grange hall (Grange P of H 533), several private dwellings, and a dam and hydroelectric plant. The Beaver River drops down out of the Adirondacks and runs by Belfort. In 1899 the first of a series of eight hydroelectric plants was opened there. The plant supplied electricity to Lowville, New York, fourteen miles away over what was, at the time, the longest electrical transmission line in the world. My father told the story of the man who appeared at the power plant one day with horse and buggy, walked down the path and into the plant and greeted the operator.

"This were they make the 'lectricity stuff?"

"It is."

"I hear tell its better'n kerosene fer light."

"'Tis."

"Got me a couple clean kerosene cans in the buggy, could I have them filled? I'd like to try it this winter."

My father, born in 1910, went to the country school. His family spoke German; he learned English in school. My mother, born in 1912, was also a student there. My three brothers and sister started school there, as did I. In the late 1940s country schools were being closed and students bused to a central school. There was a school halfway between our house and Croghan that remained open longer than any other. Most of the students came from two nearby farms where there were seventeen or eighteen children and the farmers flatly refused to allow them to go on the bus.

Lambert's Store was kitty-corner across the street, fifty yards or so from the Belfort school. The store was two stories with a concrete pad across the front, one step up from the road. A porch ran across the second-floor front. There was a Gulf gas pump out front and the building was painted white with Gulf blue and Gulf orange trim. Someone in the family had planted a lemon seed in a pot and it had grown big enough to eventually end up in a 55-gallon drum, also painted blue and orange. The tree sat on the concrete pad in the summer and was moved inside for the winter.

Clara and Walter Lambert – Clara was always named first – had living quarters in the store and raised two sons and a daughter there. Clara ran the store and Walter worked for the power company, kept a "sugarbush" – a grove of sugar maples that produced sap for maple syrup – did some hunting and fishing. Walter was slightly built, five feet five at the most, and my memory of him is that he always wore suspenders to hold up pants that must have been four to six inches too large around the waist. Clara was no taller but much, much heavier. Next door was the Peters' store, a similar operation with the Peters family living there. They also had a gas pump. Esso I think.

Our house was roughly half-a-mile from Belfort as the crow flies, not as much as twice that as the horse trots. We had to cross two bridges to go from our house to

Belfort center, the first over a gorge cut into bedrock by the river, as much as a fifty-foot drop from the bridge to the rock and water below. Right under the bridge was a wonderful kettle-hole worn into the rock by centuries of rushing water. The second bridge, fifty yards farther on, spanned the water inlet for the power plant. In recent years a canoe portage has been built around the dam, but when I was growing up there was no such thing.

Both stores sold candy, and Peters' sold ice cream on a stick and popsicles in the summer. I remember going to the store with my older brother Norman. I was next, then David. Howard and Betty came later. For our nickel we got a Three Musketeers bar. We tore open the wrapping and there were three miniature bars: chocolate covered fondant, one chocolate, one vanilla, one strawberry.

The stores stocked canned goods, bread, a few baked goods, flour, sugar, condiments, tobacco products, soaps, odds and ends. Peters' sold ammunition and hunting and fishing supplies including some bright red and black plaid jackets, before the days of Shooter's orange. Lambert's sold maple syrup from their sugarbush, and Clara kept bees and sold some honey. Rumour was that when she cleaned the penny candy counter, she put the stale candy where the bees could get to it. One year the bees got into cinnamon hearts and produced pinkish honey with a tinge of cinnamon flavor.

There was an old man living three or four miles from Belfort named Jakie Kohler. Jakie would show up at Lambert's with a burlap bag and buy groceries: several loaves of bread, six or eight cans of sweetened condensed milk for coffee, canned corned beef and Spam, sardines, salt and sugar as needed, coffee, odds and ends. Everything paid for and laid out on the counter, he proceeded to open his sack and drop his purchases in by size, bread first, followed by canned goods. Throwing the sack over his shoulder, he walked home, leaving Clara and others to wonder what the bread looked like when he got there. Peters' sold frozen confections – popsicles, Eskimo pies, and real ice cream cones.

My parents' home was next to Gospel Hall. There was a cemetery laid out around a clapboard church built on land acquired for that purpose in 1890. Built on pilings, the hall was gradually sinking into the ground. There was no official denominational affiliation. It was used for the occasional funeral, church services if a nearby minister was willing to preach for the collection – not much from a gathering of fewer than a dozen. It is where my parents are buried.

The Lamberts were the surviving trustees of the
Gospel Hall and, unable to raise money for necessary
repairs, offered it to the volunteer fire department for
practice. The Grange Hall met the same fate. Lambert's
General Store was spared. The fire chief declared it too
close to other buildings and it was torn down instead. One
theory is that Walter wanted the building burned to hide the
evidence. When the cellar was emptied out, a pile of boxes,
crates, and old furniture was dragged out to reveal said
evidence. A still was discovered along with a stock of
gallon jugs hidden behind all the detritus. The still was
vented through the chimney. Speculation was that the store
would have been a perfect front for ordering sugar, yeast,
grain, and other supplies. The store had done well during
the Depression, according to old-timers. Better than people
expected, so the gossip goes, and the still would help
explain the apparent prosperity of the family.

Walter had an automobile, but his favorite vehicle
was a 1928 Willys Overland delivery wagon, a tall machine
with wood spoked wheels useful for hauling wood and
supplies. It was his vehicle for taking supplies up to his
sugarbush and bringing out the maple syrup in drums.

The local bar, called The Nortz House, started as a
hotel of which little is known except that the original had

burned, to be replaced in 1875 by a hotel with a ballroom, dining facilities, rooms for the owners, and nine rooms upstairs. In 1977 the top floor was taken off. People such as my father and his brother, Uncle Benny, "pissed away a fortune," as one of my brothers describes it, in The Nortz House. It has since been renamed The Belfort Inn. Trudi and I decided, a few years back, to stop there on one of our visits. We walked in about ten in the morning and the woman behind the bar waved us to a table. There were four or five men at the bar, with beer, and they gave us puzzled looks, whispered a bit, and went back to drinking. The bartender came to the table and asked us what we wanted.

"Coffee," we replied.

"Oh," she said, "I can make some."

"It's all right," we said, "We don't...."

"No, no," she insisted, "I can make it." Returning to the bar, she said something and we got another round of stares and mutters. I swear I recognized a couple of the men, that they had been there since the 1940s. Maybe family resemblances.

Belfort had been quite prosperous at one time, even had its own post office. In the 1860s a tannery was built supplied with hides shipped in from South America eventually arriving in Belfort by mule train. The tanning was made possible by hemlock forest around Belfort. The trees were cut and the bark stripped and stacked, the logs being left to rot. The bark was hauled to the tannery where it was chopped, leached and the liquor put in tubs where the hides were soaked.

In 1894, the supply of bark reaching exhaustion, the tannery was closed. Irish immigrant families who had settled there to work in the tannery wandered off. A young man named Theodore Basselin (1851-1914) from nearby Croghan, just home from college, decided that leaving the logs to rot was a waste and began hiring crews to gather the logs and float them down the river to a sawmill. By the time he died, he was a millionaire (roughly $20,000,000 in 2007 purchasing value).

My father's family was not wealthy, though they did prosper as farmers. They were Amish/Mennonites, German-speaking Alsatians who immigrated to Lewis County in northern New York starting in 1832. My father was born in 1910. His name was Ruben, though it was sometimes spelled Reuben. Most people called him Rudy. There seemed to have been some intention to name him Rudolph and the doctor who delivered him may have filled out the birth certificate wrongly.

He was the youngest of eight children, one of whom had died in adolescence. His father, Daniel, was a tall man, much in contrast to my father's mother, Fannie, who was short. Daniel and Fannie were married in November 1897. They lived on the family farm all their lives, Daniel dying in 1933 at age fifty-seven. Fannie lived until 1970, age ninety-three. My father died at Christmas time in 1956, and I remember Fannie standing by his grave saying that it was not fair; children were supposed to bury their parents and she had already buried children.

My mother, Leona Marolf, started life on a farm a couple of miles down the road toward Croghan. At some point, her parents moved to Carthage, New York, where her father, Edward, took a job in a feed mill. Her mother, Ida, was a housewife. They had three other children in addition to my mother: Aunt Ruthie, Uncle Robbie, and a son who died in his teens.

The custom was for children to quit school and go to work as early as the law allowed. Their parents expected to collect their children's wages – really generous parents would allow the children to keep half their pay – usually until the child was eighteen, sometimes even twenty-one. My parents both left school as soon as the law allowed, age fourteen in their day, although my mother had done well in school and tried unsuccessfully to convince her parents to allow her to graduate. My mother went to work as a domestic with a farm family, my father to work on the farm.

As a teen, my father was something of a "rake-hell." He owned a Ford runabout, a Model T two-seater. About the only thing I clearly remember him saying about the car was that he could outrun anything the state police could put on the road in that part of the world, and they never caught him. Rudy had a drinking problem all of his life – not a steady drunk, nor a mean one, but a binge drinker. He'd stop at a bar anytime he had money, including his paycheck, and celebrate. Our mother often had to deal with him coming home late on payday with all of his money gone.

Daniel, my father's father, also had a drinking problem, according to family memories. He would buy a wagon load of grapes every fall from a peddler and make wine in barrels in the cellar. Then he'd go to church and kneel before the pulpit praying to be freed of his sin. The congregation would pray for him, the ministers would lay hands on him, and he would go home, go down cellar and begin drinking. My father told of Fannie sitting by Daniel's bed as he died and, when he breathed his last, covering his face with the sheet and going down cellar to knock the bungs out of his barrels, saving one gallon for "medicinal purposes." The cellar had a dirt floor, and my father remembered the smell permeating the house for a year. The so-called medicinal wine went to my father's brother, Uncle Benny, for his wife, who was dying of tuberculosis.

Uncle Benny was a woodsman who made a business during World War II of providing venison for people without the necessity of using meat ration coupons. After my grandmother died, Uncle Benny got a job at what had been a CCC camp, taken over by 4H, where he taught woodcraft, hunting, the skills of foresters. He mentored a generation of youths and was so well-liked and admired that they named the administration building after him.

The Widrick side of the family was rather strict about photographs. Grandma Widrick would get angry if you even pointed a camera in her direction. There was a picture of my father as a teenager with his pet bull. Though it was a large animal, my father had managed to train it and got along well with it. When it came time in the late afternoon to bring in the cows for milking, he would get out the bull, tie a rope to the ring in its nose, mount up, and ride the bull off to the round-up.

My father found various ways to make a living: worked for my grandmother on the family farm, was a lumberjack, sometimes cooked in a lumber camp (he was a good cook), worked off and on in paper mills (he hated the regular hours he was expected to keep) and during hunting season worked at hunting camps as a guide. I later had an orthopedic surgeon in Syracuse, New York, who knew him from hunting camp, and in about 1989 I ran into a parishioner in Auburn, New York, whose father recognized the name from the same hunting camp.

Rudy's last job was working for his brother, my Uncle Daniel. Dannie had a farm and ran a butcher shop. There they slaughtered animals, sold meat retail, butchered for other people, cured hams and bacon and made sausages of various types. One bright morning in October 1956 my father left home headed for Dannie's. A neighbor working near the road waved at him as he drove by.

Rudy liked to sing as he drove; it was a warm day so he had the car window down. The neighbor recalled him singing the familiar words, "When the trumpet of the Lord shall sound, and time shall be more, / And the morning breaks, eternal, bright and fair; / When the saved of earth shall gather over on the other shore, / And the roll is called up yonder, I'll be there. . . ." fading away in the distance.

He got to work and went out to the smoke house to boil rings of bologna preparatory to smoking them. He was careless with fire – I remember him burning trash at home in a barrel, lighting fires in the wood stove, burning brush piles. If the fire did not perform the way he wanted it to, he would douse it with kerosene and grin as the fire exploded.

The smoke house fire must have been too slow for him; he picked up a gallon can, the old metal kind with a screw top and a spout on the side used to carry kerosene and old crank case oil for fires. Later it was believed, though no one would admit it, that someone had recently carried gasoline in the same can. He apparently threw some of the contents on the fire. The stream burst into flame and the can exploded, blowing open about a third of the bottom seam so that several quarts of flaming kerosene and oil, and perhaps some gas, blew out toward him and caught him in the stomach.

He ran for help, struggling to tear off his clothing. Dannie knocked him down and rolled him on the ground. Bishop Lloyd Boshart of the Mennonite church, who was driving in, rushed over and knelt beside him. My father spoke with the bishop in his native German, and from then on spoke little English ever again.

Boshart accompanied Rudy to the hospital. As soon as they had him stabilized, he was transferred to the University Hospital in Syracuse, New York. Massive third-, fourth-, fifth- and even sixth-degree burns covered his body; on parts of his right arm and hands the flesh was burned away to the bone. The hospital staff fought a valiant but losing battle, wrapping his legs in bandages with little tubes sticking out into which they injected something to keep the raw flesh moist. A few small skin grafts were attempted, but he there wasn't a lot of healthy skin left to take the grafts from.

Shortly before he died, the hospital had family members sign papers volunteering to donate skin grafts if our blood types matched. Apparently there was not much hope of long-term success, but they were trying to buy time to let his body heal as much as it could. Being a woodsman, Rudy was aware that girdling a tree – removing a strip of bark from around its entire circumference – would kill it, and in a period of lucidity he asked my mother to check under his bandages to see whether he had been "girdled." He had not, to his great relief. And being a man, he asked her one day to check under the covers to make certain that his "private parts" had not been lost, since the catheter

15

made him unaware of urine passing. He died after two months in the hospital, on the 20th of December.

Rudy was laid out in our living room, and his brother-in-law Elias Zehr, a Bishop of the Mennonite church, a kind and remarkable man, conducted his funeral service right there at home. Rudy was buried next door to our home in the Gospel Hall Cemetery.

"Tuffy" Dicoup (pronounced "Dee Cup"), who had worked in the woods with Rudy, guided hunters with him, and spent a lot of time drinking with him, was among the guests who came to the calling hours, carrying his own pint of brandy with him. One of Rudy's favorite stories had been about how Tuffy had shot a deer, in season which was a bit unusual for him, but without antlers. As he was hauling the deer down a logging road, a game warden stepped out and demanded to see his hunting license and then, looking at the deer, said, "That's not a buck."

"Got balls, ain't it?" Tuffy replied and hauled the deer off.

Tuffy and I talked into the night about the woods and hunting and friendship. He told me a story I had never heard in which he and Rudy were guiding at a hunting camp one autumn. Late in the afternoon – late in the sense that the sun was low in the sky – most of the men were back at the camp putting away rifles and ammunition when they heard shots. Tuffy and Rudy together started off towards the shots to meet one of their hunters.

"We heard shots," they told him.

"Yeah, I think I hit a bear," the man answered.

"Where the hell is it?"

"Ran off into brush."

"Get back to camp," Rudy grumbled. The two of them followed the trail until they smelled gunpowder and found clots of blood on some bushes. Then they trailed the wounded beast into a swampy area. There was a sudden roar, and the bear reared up in front of them.

"Stand behind me," Rudy said, "and be ready to shoot." Then he stepped forward, held his rifle at waist height and fired. The bear lunged forward and Rudy fired off all five rounds in his rifle. The bear pitched forward and slashed with a paw. Dead, his claws, according to Tuffy, were less than half an inch from the tip of Rudy's boot.

Back at the camp, Rudy walked up to the man who had first shot the bear. "You can't leave a wounded animal like that, and, dammit, not a wounded bear," Rudy told him. "It could kill somebody. You get your gear packed and you get the hell out of this camp tomorrow at dawn, and don't you ever let me see your face around here again."

As Tuffy got ready to leave our home that night, he drew me out onto the back porch and said, "You tell your ma I got me a couple a deer hanging in the woods and she can have all the venison she wants."

We buried Rudy the 23rd of December, 1956, leaving Christmas always a sad time in my memory.

My mother was a good cook, though she tended to rely on frying things. To cook bacon, she heated a frying pan, threw in a gob of lard, and, when it was hot enough, put in the bacon. But her cakes and pies were excellent, and she was fast and efficient. She canned massive amounts of food: corn, beans, peas, carrots, meat, pickles, jams and jellies. I still crave her pickled beets with a few cloves in the jar. Or dilly beans.

My mother was hospitalized for several weeks in the fall of 1950 and my father decided to make dill pickles. He sometimes experimented, as in the case of the year when he trapped beaver and decided that beaver burgers would be yummy. We learned that they are not; their meat tastes bitter from the tree bark they eat. Helping my father in his quest to make dill pickles, we went out to the garden and found some horseradish growing near a fence, something we never used. But we dug up some roots and dad put a spear of horseradish in each of about two dozen jars of dill pickles. Mom recovered and came home from the hospital but never forgave him the horseradish. The rest of us liked those pickles.

Leona died in June 1971 following gall bladder surgery. When we cleaned out the house and divided up its contents prior to my brother Howard buying it, we found jars of jams and jellies on the cellar shelves so old that the sugar had crystallized. We also found quart jars of blackberries she had put up in 1948 – the solids had separated from the liquids and settled to the bottoms of the jars, but the jars were still sealed.

The first cars in the Mennonite community were black, with black paint on all of the chrome work and no radios. Electricity had come relatively early to the area by way of the Belfort Power Plant, and that didn't seem to conflict with anyone's beliefs, though in the 1950s some Mennonites got involved in a more conservative movement and had their electric service disconnected. Their objection was not to electricity but to being billed for the electricity. They wanted cash and carry, not carry and cash.

Belfort, the place of my childhood, is a way of life. It is reflected in dark clothing, women with bonnets and no makeup, men without neckties. It was a simple life, we claimed, though no life is simple; but we meant that we did not do much "just for pretty" as my Aunt Esther, Rudy's sister, would say. Or, truth to tell, we avoided admitting that it was "just for pretty."

One of my favorite paintings is Salvador Dalí's *The Persistence of Memory,* a fantastic landscape with clocks and watches, but the clocks and watches are fluid and always look to me like eggs as they pour out of the shell, running off the edge of a table, draped over a branch. Time flows and distorts. How much of what I recall is true, sixty years and more later?

I remember the measles, when we had to stay in a room with the shades drawn because the light might hurt our eyes. I remember my brother making mashed potato sandwiches with white bread, a layer of potato, mayonnaise. I remember that we found some axel grease and played with it, then tried to clean our hands by wiping them on the clapboards of the house and got spanked. I remember being in my maternal grandparents' kitchen when a man dressed in an Army uniform came to visit. He let me play with his hat, which had a celluloid panel sewn into the crown, and he showed my grandfather pictures of himself in what I was to later learn was a French Foreign Legion uniform – but my aunt, who was also there, told me when I asked a few years ago that that it never happened.

I remember too a time my father came home with a box of groceries and my mother looked in the box and asked, "Where are they?"

"What?" he asked.

"My cigarettes," she replied, and they yelled at each other for a while. Much later, as an adult in the process of quitting smoking myself, I mentioned that memory to her and said I knew she could appreciate how difficult it was.

"I never smoked," she said.

"Yes, you did."

"No, I never did."

Another liquid Dalí watch dripping off a window sill.

The American humorist and cartoonist James Thurber (1894-1961) is quoted as having said, "Love is what we have been through together." What we have been through. Together. I don't suppose our memories have to be all that accurate. Time has flowed. This is what we have been through together.

There are still pieces of mythology in my memory that I would like to recheck. I have it set in my mind that the Old Order Amish Church in Croghan, New York, which my grandparents belonged to buries people by date. Behind the church is the burying ground with rows and rows of small markers. There are no family plots. Everyone is buried in turn, which would leave my grandparents buried thirty-seven years apart.

It seems rather nice, noting the separation of time, the years that passed without each other, honoring the flow of time. I decided one day that if I moved back there and apologized to the church elders for leaving, they might let me have a space when my time comes. But I don't even know if the burial arrangement is what I think it is, and, as old Tom Wolfe so aptly put it, "You can't go home again." Still, we went through our lives together, if only for a time, and that is the essence and the presence of love.

~2~

1932-1938: Belfort, New York

I was born on September 26th, 1932, close to midnight. My mother's birthday was September 27th, and the attending physician offered to alter my birth certificate such that it would say I was born on my mother's birthday. She turned down the offer.

At the time of my birth, my parents were living with my grandmother during my father's brief stint running the family farm. Some of my earliest memories are of living there with my parents and my older brother Norman and younger brother David. My Aunt Esther lived there too. I remember walking behind my father as he plowed with a team of horses, me with a tin can picking up worms. Attached is the memory of a bucket kept in the cellar filled with earth where the worms were kept until needed for fishing. Dad would sometimes sprinkle cornmeal in the bucket to feed the worms. In another memory, Norman and

I were mashing dandelions with a hammer and I somehow ended up bopping him on the head with it.

I also remember the day that I became aware that people could do something I later learned was called "counting." I went into the kitchen and saw a mesh basket of eggs sitting on the counter by the sink. I had a mud-pie project out behind the barn and thought that a few eggs would improve the mix inasmuch as eggs were used in cakes and other baked goods. I filled my pockets and went off to my "bakery." Much pleased with the results of the egg and mud recipe, I returned to the house, only to be asked what I had done with the eggs. I lied, proclaiming my innocence. But they knew that eggs were missing and I was punished. The fact that the basket still looked full to me and yet somehow there was a way the adults had of knowing that some of the eggs were gone was my first inkling of the concept of counting.

This was Mennonite country. Horse and buggy was still a common means of transportation in those parts at that time, although my family had a car for as long as I can remember. Every Sunday, my whole family attended services at the Mennonite church six or seven miles from our home. Women and men sat on separate sides of the church, and we sang with nothing more than a pitch pipe to accompany us.

Christmas was a big cause for celebration in my childhood home. One year when my father was working at a lumber camp, he drove home with a blue spruce tied to the roof of his car. My mother went into town and bought a box of blue lights to decorate it with – something she'd always wanted to do. On Christmas morning, my brothers and sister and I would usually find our stockings filled with nuts, hard candies, oranges, socks, mittens, clothing. One year my brother Norman and I both received dump trucks. We'd have Christmas dinner at my paternal grandparents' farm: a potluck with venison, bird, beef, potatoes, whatever the various participants had on hand to bring.

Birthdays were not huge occasions in my childhood, but we still managed to celebrate despite having little money for presents. During the years we lived at my grandparents' farm, I remember being presented with a chocolate cake with candles on it. A more peculiar birthday memory I have involves standing on the kitchen table at the farm while my mother and an aunt pinned a crepe paper gown on me. I never had the opportunity to ask anyone in my family about that odd random memory, but years later, in college, I was reading about folk customs and learned that in some areas of Germany it was once the custom to dress little boys as girls on their birthdays to protect them from being stolen by wood fairies. So maybe that explains my strange birthday memory.

When I was about five or six years old, my parents bought their own house and we moved off the farm. We were located next to Gospel Hall on Belfort Road, which ran from Belfort about four or five miles to Croghan. The road followed a plateau which dropped away to a stretch of flat land and the river. Our house was about a hundred yards from where the land began to drop.

At the age of six I started attending the country school, a one-room schoolhouse with about a dozen kids from age six to fourteen. My father had attended the same school as a child. I remember little about that school except that it had very tall windows, and at the very top of one of the tall windows was an apple that had become embedded when some kid threw it and it broke the glass but lodged in place. The schoolhouse was heated by a wood stove, and we carried buckets of water to school. I also remember a large play yard with a swing and a side. If we wanted to use the slide we had to protect our pants with the waxed paper that bread loaves came wrapped in, or our parents would complain about the wear and tear to our clothes.

~3~

1939-1947: Watertown and Oneonta

St. Ignatius of Loyola had, as one of the goals of his spiritual exercises, the intention that we learn that each of us is a personality deformed by our past. I find the description apt. I suppose that, in Ignatius' terms, an odyssey is a story of spiritual formation. Deformity is a part of that formation, those things we have to live with, change, work around, carry with us from the past as we live into the future.

One of the realities and blessings of life is that we can invent and reinvent ourselves. I discussed this at one time with a therapist, and we concluded that inventing ourselves was not always so bad; it can be a way of surviving.

As an adult I sat down at home in front of a fire one cold wet Saturday afternoon, the family all out doing other things, to read Gloria Steinem's book about Marilyn Monroe. She wrote of Marilyn, at the age of seven, being left at an orphanage, her family no longer able to take care of her. Reading the passage opened – not a floodgate – but a leak in my heart and soul, and I began to cry. The experience of abandonment, of pain, the loneliness – long carefully put away in the interest of survival – were all too real.

My childhood ended when I was seven, or, more accurately, seven years and one month within a few days. I was not placed in an orphanage. I was placed in a hospital, and part of the bitterness was realizing that I had accepted the intellectual fact that it was for my "own good." (Isn't there an Eastern curse which goes "May someone do good to you"?)

Following these Saturday tears inspired by Marilyn Monroe, to whom I now see I owe a debt of gratitude, I called a therapist with whom we had worked in the past over personal and family issues, and made an appointment to talk about it.

Self-analysis is usually faulty, but my faulty sense of self now is that I was stuck somewhere between detachment and depression (if we look at stage models), and somehow along the way never got to express the anger which is so much a part of loss.

By the time I was seven, I had a well-developed case of Pott's disease. Sir Percival Pott (1714-1788) was a London surgeon. Following an accident he devoted a lengthy recuperation to writing, describing various diseases and conditions. Pott's disease was so named from his description. The more scientific term is tuberculosis spondylodiscitis, tuberculosis of the spine. The poet Alexander Pope suffered from Pott's disease. The classic hunchback or humpback was often the result of Pott's disease.

I remember my father taking me to a doctor. When we got home he had me stand against a door frame and try to straighten up to show my mother what had happened to me. "He can't live like that," my father declared. "I might as well take him out and shoot him."

My childhood predated mandatory Tuberculin testing for milk cows. Somewhere along the line it was suggested to me that I had probably contracted Bovine Tuberculosis from drinking milk or eating undercooked meat from infected animals. I have no idea how long the spinal curvature had been developing by the time it was diagnosed. We used to have a photograph of me standing between my older brother Norman and my younger brother David in front of a large maple tree on the family farm. They had smiles on their faces, but there was no way of telling whether or not I was smiling: my head was dropped down with the crown showing – still my favored position. So already the curvature was in evidence then.

As a young boy, I stayed with my maternal grandparents, Ed and Ida Marolf, in Carthage, New York, for long periods of time. I had a room to myself in their large Victorian house, as well as clothing and toys there that I did not have at home. The Marolfs belonged to a small and wonderful Church of the Nazarene. We went to evening services. I would sit next to my grandmother, who fed me Lifesavers to keep me quiet. I remember her wearing a dress, black with a layer of purple gauze over it. The minister would lead the hymns, and sometimes when a hymn was finished he would call out, "I like that one, let's sing it again!" And they did.

When the time in the service came for prayers for healing, my grandmother would take me to the altar. I would kneel and she would kneel beside me. The minister would lay his hands on my head and pray while my grandmother quietly sobbed, "Oh, Jesus. Oh, Jesus...."

Then we would return to our pew and she would get out the Lifesavers.

The year I was seven, I was taken for x-rays. I had no comprehension of what was happening except for the memory of seeing the x-rays, mysterious sheets of dark which my parents and other relatives held up to the light, whispering about what they revealed. What I remember best is that on one of the mysterious trips to see doctors and have x-rays, my grandmother took me to an ice cream shop that sold the double cones with two scopes side by side, and for some reason halfway through the ice cream I decided to bite the bottom off the cone. Melted ice cream dripped out onto me and onto the glass top of our table, making a mess.

Years later, my mother told me that she had wanted to take me to a "faith healer" who had a following in that part of New York state, but my grandparents apparently took control of the situation. In October 1939, just after I turned seven years old – I believe it was October 20th – I was admitted to the Jefferson County Sanatorium in Watertown, New York. Looking through my file years later, while the doctor was out of the room, I found a court order making me a ward of the state and ordering medical treatment. (Thank you, New York.)

The treatment for Tb at the time was time. There were no effective drugs or antibiotics, and one simply waited to get better, or not. I was taken to the hospital, put in pajamas, put in bed on a frame, an oblong construction of pipe with canvas stretched over it and a jacket to hold me in place, told to be good and assured that they – my grandparents and mother – would be back in a week.

The jacket held my chest and shoulders down. I think I just crawled into the jacket which had arm and head holes. I don't recall buckles or ties or buttons. There was a head harness, a halter attached to a weight by a rope which ran through a pulley at the head of the bed. Later a box was added to the bed to hold the sheet and blankets up off my feet.

It is vague: my memory is that I was a very passive patient, something that I find hard to believe in retrospect. I must have been upset, felt abandoned, overwhelmed by being dropped into this strange world and confined to bed. I think my grandparents and mother came back the following Saturday and a few more times, but the longer I was there the farther apart the visits. I have been told that I must have been in a great deal of pain. I do not remember that. I do remember the sense of abandonment – it is with me always.

In retrospect I think I "shut down." Something I still do as a way of dealing with stress.

Someone from the maintenance department took a hospital bed tray, one of those adjustable things on wheels, and attached a mirror to it so that, lying flat on my back, I could see the top of the tray in reflection. I learned to eat that way: backwards or upside down. Rather messy at first but eventually I became adept at it.

I had a roommate named Gerald, who was a few years older than me. Our two person room was separated from the corridor by a larger room with beds for four patients. The standard treatment along with rest was plenty of fresh air, and our room had one wall lined with windows. Gerald was allowed to get up and walk about, go to the bathroom. Eventually he was discharged, but a few months later one of the nurses told me that he had been readmitted. I thought it would be nice to get my roommate back. And then the news – he had been badly bruised, and the site of the bruise developed into a tuberculosis infection which spread rapidly through his bloodstream – miliary tuberculosis. It was almost always fatal in those days before antibiotics, and it was for Gerald as well.

My memory of that time has been reduced to bits and pieces, what have been called "shards of memory," much faded and distorted by time. One night a nurse came into my room to turn out the lights and check me out. As she left, she asked me if I had remembered to say my prayers. My Grandmother Marolf had taught me "Now I lay me down to sleep," and I was pretty consistent about it, so I said I would. Then she looked at me and said, "Be sure you ask God to forgive you."

"Forgive me for what?" I asked wondering what I had done wrong that she knew about.

"I don't know," she said, "but you must have done something very, very bad to be as sick as you are."

I would have been nine or ten at the time. I was stunned. How could I, strapped to a frame, have done something "very, very bad"? It took me a long time to get over that incident.

The hospital did make provisions for the education of children. I learned to read and write. (I still remember "Dick, see Dick, see Dick run. Run, Dick, run.") And always fresh in my mind was my early confusion between the spelling of homophones "one" and "won." But Sunday School, religious education, was not part of the official program. Several years later, however, we had some Cadet nurses working at the hospital. They wore blue uniforms and Caduceus lapel pins, and two of them decided that we needed a Sunday School. On Sunday mornings we would be taken to the hospital classroom and they would read to us, tell stories, and teach us songs. One of the songs referred to being "in the King's army." After singing it one Sunday, one of the Cadets asked if we knew what it meant to be "in the King's army." Saturated with news of World War II, I responded, "The British army!"

Patients were not allowed radios, but the rooms were wired for earphones with wall plugs equipped with a volume control and a switch to allow access to several radio stations, chosen and controlled from – if memory serves – the central telephone switchboard. The receivers were turned on in the morning and turned off at 10 or 11 at night. I listened to a lot of radio programs: Arturo Toscanini and the NBC Symphony, Soap Operas (*One Man's Family, Stella Dallas, Backstage Wife,* and on and on), comedy (*Jack Benny, Bob Hope, Fibber McGee and Molly, Baby Snooks,* amongst others), adventure series (*The Lone Ranger* was a favorite), and the news. I remember the announcement of the bombing of Pearl Harbor.

I was in the Jefferson County Sanatorium for a few years. Sometime in 1942 or 1943 it was decided (by whom? We were never told such things; decisions were made somewhere and our lives changed) that I would be moved to the state-run Homer Folks Hospital in Oneonta, New York. A nurse came into my room and announced that my few possessions had been packed, and I was loaded into an ambulance and sent on my way. No goodbyes, no chance to tell people that I would miss them, no leave-taking, just moved.

Homer Folks was much larger, with six buildings and a whole wing dedicated to children (anyone under the age of eighteen, I would guess, from the people I remember being there). The hospital did not provide us with much in the way of personal space. We had a bed, a bedstand, and a nightstand. Toys not being played with and books not being read were stored in a large closet nearby.

One of the things that little boys collected was lead soldiers, even bedridden little boys. I had a small collection, and even better, some cowboys and Indians, the Lone Ranger on his white horse among them. One day I asked for my lead soldiers (which were kept in a grape basket) and the nurse came back to tell me that they were not there. I complained and she went back and looked again, and then got the head nurse. My lead soldiers were gone. In fact, all the metal toys that had been in the closet turned out to be missing. It took only a short time for the terrible truth to be revealed. One of the night nurses had decided it was her patriotic duty to contribute to a scrap metal drive, and she had packed up all of the metal toys she could find in the closet and dropped them off on her way home in the morning. Protests and tears and attempts by hospital staff to recover the toys were in vain. The lead soldiers, the dancing ballerina top, the tin cars were all lost. Many years after, I read that the scrap metal drives were mostly a propaganda stunt – it was too expensive and time-consuming to sort the metal, and what was collected went to a dump.

The Homer Folks Hospital, named in honor of Homer Folks (1867-1963), who was a leader in social reform, public health issues, care of children, and relief of poverty, was run by the state of New York. Tuberculosis was a massive public health problem before antibiotics, and government on various levels was involved in trying to treat and control what was known as "the white plague." During warm weather, those of us confined to beds would be wheeled out onto a large wooden deck for fresh air and sunshine. In the winter, there was a room with some kind of sunlamp under which we would be put on a regular basis. There was a large classroom to which we were taken for lessons.

At some point the children's wing was closed, and I was placed in a private room in an adult wing. The rest of the children must have been sent to other hospitals, as I no longer saw them around. I was briefly returned to the children's wing after developing something along the lines of pneumonia or flu which required me to be separated from the other patients. I really don't remember much except that I think that I was in an oxygen tent for a time, and then later returned to my regular room.

Death in the sanatorium was both arbitrary and common. Surviving patients were given no help with mourning or grief: Death was not spoken of beyond the informational necessities. Tb of the lungs can be a devastating disease. Before antibiotics, there was no treatment other than time and sometimes rather brutal surgery. There is a procedure called a thoracoplasty which involves the surgical removal of ribs in order to collapse a lung. Immobile, the lung tissue could form calcified areas and confine the tuberculosis infection.

Pulmonary tuberculosis usually resulted in the coughing up of a great deal of sputum. As the infection destroyed more tissue, bleeding was common. The patients were supplied with sputum cups, and the daily production was recorded. Sputum with blood in it was worrisome, and in many cases a major bleed in the lung led to death. Discharge from the hospital came with a negative finding of Tb bacillus by microscopic examination of the sputum for a certain period of time.

Sputum cups were commonly kept at the bedside. The cups were made of waxed cardboard, about the size of Chinese take-out containers with a lid. There were also pocket cups that ambulatory patients could carry with them. One of my activities was the folding of cups. Patients usually folded their own, but the staff liked to have extra cups prepared, and some of us took on that task.

The state of New York, at that time, apparently had strict laws regarding treatment of tuberculosis, which was one of the leading causes of death until well into the twentieth century. I recall one man delivered to the hospital in a straitjacket by the state police. I'm not sure what happened to him after his arrival.

People on the nursing staff provided me with newspapers: sometimes the *New York Times*, often the *New York Daily News* (as much of a rag then as now), and magazines. My favorites were *Popular Science* and *Popular Mechanics*. World War II was raging, and these two magazines were full of information about weapons and explosives and interesting things like delayed action fuses on shells. And, of course, airplane identification. The chances of a German or Japanese plane flying over New York state were infinitesimal, but I studied silhouette charts and learned the names and designation of combat aircraft. The P38 with twin tail booms was a favorite; I attempted to build a model with balsa wood and tissue paper, but it came out pretty strange and I think I never finished it.

I did my first year of high school in the hospital. One of my fellow patients was a high school math teacher. He was a Christian Scientist and rather upset about having to be there since he had faith that Christian Science would cure him. But the state law was that his teaching credentials were suspended until he was pronounced cured or in remission by the hospital authorities. His fiancée would visit every Sunday, and they read together from *Science and Health with Key to the Scriptures*, Mary Baker Eddy's primary text about Christian Science and its biblical foundation for healing. He did get better faster than most people.

I had a private room at the time, and other patients with lung infections were allowed to visit with me by pulling a chair up to my door, though they were not allowed any closer for fear of contagion. One regular visitor was Nat White, a pleasant young man who sat in the doorway and taught me about the metric system. In that way I learned centimeters and millimeters and kilograms.

We were a mixed crowd, and many of my fellow patients have stayed in my mind over the years. There was a Swiss woman named Hilda Vogelsang who became trapped in New York by the war. She might have been able to get home to Switzerland after the surrender of France, but she was Jewish and afraid to try to cross German-occupied France or Vichy France even with her Swiss passport.

A tall, slender woman with copper-colored hair was always called the Greek Girl. Her boyfriend would visit her, bringing bags of onions which she peeled and ate the way people eat apples, offering them to other patients also. By whatever process such decisions were made, it was decided she was a candidate for a thoracoplasty and the operation was performed. We never had much time to think about such things: the patients were told of a decision and the procedure was done. Later I heard a physician refer to this practice as "Imperial medicine."

After the Greek Girl's operation, she was returned to her ward and put in bed on her side, operation site down, to prevent the fluid from draining into her good lung. She was essentially sandbagged into that position. Somehow she managed to free herself from the sandbags and turn over on her other side during the night. By the next morning, she had developed pneumonia. She died that afternoon.

Another fellow patient was Mr. Pettit, probably in his seventies, whose daughter was in the same hospital in the women's ward, both of them having been simultaneously diagnosed with Tb. Mr. Pettit got up early every morning and dressed himself in a three-piece suit with a gold watch chain on his vest. I have no idea what he had done for a living, but he would tell wonderful stories about the Philippines Insurrection (1899-1902), in which he served in the U. S. Army. I remember his descriptions of Moro guerillas rushing out of concealed positions to attack American soldiers with machetes.

There was a man from someplace in Central America or the Caribbean, possibly the Dominican Republic. He had Tb in his right shoulder joint, an open sore which was treated by his spending as much time as possible exposing the sore to the sun. I think that he viewed his condition as an excellent excuse for not going home, where he was apparently wanted for some political problems. His wife would sit by him while he sunned, reading him books and papers.

And there was a man who was an undertaker by profession. Although he was pleasant and sociable, most of the other patients treated him badly. I think his profession was too close to home for us.

Those who did not die were discharged or moved without any advance word, and for those of us left behind they seemed to simply disappear. An ethnic Japanese woman entered the sanatorium one day. She came from California, but they could not hospitalize her there – ethnic Japanese on the West Coast were being incarcerated in concentration camps during the war, and apparently even one Japanese was seen as a danger, so she was shipped to New York state for treatment.

We had an orderly named Freddie Schwartz. One of the nurses referred to him as an "ordament." Freddie was a veteran of WWI, German Army. He fought on the Russian front. As Germany collapsed in the closing months of that war, military units mutinied, and Freddie's was one of those. The mutiny started in naval units, and ships and bases were seized by sailors who ran up the red flag and proclaimed Communist loyalties.

Freddie told of how his Army unit voted to join with sailors at a base and their commanding officer stood on a table and ordered them back to their positions.

Someone threw a steel helmet at him and dozens of other men joined in. Then they marched off to join the revolution. He had a wonderful collection of bank notes promising to be redeemable in gold after the war and told stories of serving as a machine gunner in the Freikorps and the desperation of the hyperinflation of the 1920s.

In September of 1945, shortly after the end of the war and just before my thirteenth birthday, the invisible powers that be decided that I was to undergo surgery. I was transported by ambulance – not the kind with sirens but one of those ambulances owned by a funeral parlor, with a lot of chrome and the name of the establishment on the windows – to the University Hospital in Syracuse, New York (now part of the State University of New York). The surgeon was a Dr. Severance who, I soon learned, had known my father back when my father worked as a hunting guide at a camp in the Adirondacks where Dr. Severance was a regular visitor.

After Dr. Severance performed a spinal fusion involving five vertebrae, I had what I later heard described as a "near death" experience. I was on the operating table for about six hours and apparently bled a lot. The college-aged daughter of one of the cleaning women at the hospital, in response to the depletion of the blood supply that resulted from my situation, rounded up fifteen or twenty fellow students at Syracuse University to donate blood in my name.

Later I was told that at one point during the operation, the attending staff thought I was dead. What I remember is that I was given ether and had the sensation of falling upward through a tunnel toward light. My next memory is of waking up on a bed with the distinct sensation that I had fallen a great distance and landed hard. That sensation of falling has never left me. When I awoke, it was early morning and a doctor was offering me an injection for the pain while a blood transfusion line was running into my ankle.

I stayed there only a few weeks before being transferred to a nearby sanatorium, and eventually back to Oneonta for recovery. A nurse asked me during that time what I wanted to do once I finished school. I said something about wanting to be an airplane designer. The nurse grew very concerned by this answer and explained that I needed to plan on a desk job because I would never walk normally again. That was news to me!

I spent the next several months in a wheelchair, eventually becoming quite able with it. For about a year I was encased in a plaster cast, neck to hips; then a back brace; and then finally I began exercises to get me up on my feet. I was fifteen years old and learning to walk – but the nurse's prognostication was wrong, and in time I did walk normally again.

~4~

1948-1952: Returning to Belfort

Throughout all those years I spent in hospitals as a child, I had been able to maintain a mythology about my family – that that were happy, they would be glad to have me home, they did not come to see me because of the war (gas rationing was part of life). I would be happy when I got home.

But when the time came, going home was difficult. As had been the case with all the other hospital patients I knew who left, the timing seemed arbitrary. I'd witnessed the sequence many times: An X-ray was taken, a sputum test turned out negative, a patient was declared in remission, and a nurse would be instructed to tell the patient, "You can go home now." Most did not wait around but left as soon as transportation could be arranged.

In August of 1948, my parents somehow got the idea that I was to go home for a visit. I was not informed of the event, and, so far as I could tell from the confusion, neither were the people on duty that day. My father showed up in the expectation that I was to go home with him for a few weeks' visit. When he arrived, phone calls had to be made to someone in authority, and the word came back that since someone was there to pick me up, I might as well be discharged. This took about two hours, as I recall, and then I was in the back seat of a car, leaving behind what had been my home and family for nine years.

With no opportunity to say goodbye or to express the grief and fear I was feeling, I was going home, the happy wish of every patient there – even the ones who had been in one sanatorium or another twenty years or more. There is another Eastern curse: "May all of your wishes be granted." How could I then think (or worse, say) that I did not want to go home?

I am not certain how much of what was happening at home I knew about. I don't recall it being any surprise, so I must have had some awareness of it. Perhaps the occasional letter or visit had given me some indication (when I say occasional, I am referring to two, maybe three, visits or letters a year). I knew, for instance, that there had been a rift between my parents and my father's family. I had had a letter from my mother about some argument she had had with an aunt and uncle. Why did she write to me about it? I never can quite imagine.

My mother was not a happy person much of the time. Being poor in rural northern New York in the 1940s was certainly no easier than anywhere else, and my parents were not happy together. My father dealt with the problem by being away a lot working and by drinking too much. My mother responded to just about every disagreement and issue with verbal abuse.

I arrived home feeling utterly disenfranchised. There I was, far out in the countryside, surrounded by people in Mennonite dress. I was a stranger to my family. I hadn't seen my three brothers or my sister in nearly a decade. Suddenly I needed to get to know these people as family. It was bewildering. All of my dreams, hopes, illusions, wishes, memories, and plans for home were scattered by reality.

I made some attempts to get back into the religious world of the Mennonites, attending revival meetings which always raised more questions than they answered. If God were just, why did we get treated so badly? I did learn one valuable lesson one hot summer's night. The preacher went on and on and on, then finally pointed out that the hour was getting late and he had noticed that some people were looking at the wall clock or sneaking peeks at watches. That meant they were not saved yet, since they were bored with the word of God, so he was going to continue until they had heard the message. No more peeks at the time.

When summer ended, I headed off for the first time to Beaver River Central School in Beaver Falls, just like any other kid my age would. It was a half-hour ride by school bus. It was a small school, just eighteen or so per grade. I didn't know any of the other students, and it took a while to feel acclimated, but eventually I made a few friends, boys who were nonathletic like me and were excluded from the clique of jocks.

Gradually I grew stronger and my walking abilities improved. Academically I had no trouble fitting in. My eclectic education in the hospital had served me well; I'd even learned geometry. The only thing that was new to me was Latin, which all high schoolers were required to take for two years.

College was not the typical path in my family. My oldest brother had followed the Mennonite tradition of quitting school at sixteen to become a farmer. My brother David went into the Army for two years and then attended a two-year college program, after which he had a good career as a lab technician for Bristol Myers in Syracuse. My youngest brother, Howard, quit school at sixteen and became something of a hell-raiser. My sister Betty graduated from high school but never went to college.

But my medical condition and the fact that I was a ward of the state qualified me for New York's rehabilitation program, through which I could attend college, the idea being that someone like me could never expect to earn a living through farming or other manual labor so I'd better learn to do something to support myself. And I qualified through standardized testing for a Regent's Scholarship. After considering a few different options among the state schools, I chose Potsdam State College, which is now SUNY Potsdam but was then a teacher training college, and in the fall of 1950 I left Belfort once again – this time to move into a freshman dorm at Potsdam State.

~ 5~

1951-1955: Potsdam

Just as when I started high school, I knew no one at
college and had to make all new friends, but I actually
enjoyed it. I liked the exposure to books and learning that
college fostered, and I liked the people I was meeting. My
three roommates and I got along well, and I found my
classes interesting. I was discovering that I felt comfortable
within the structure of institutions, which hearkens back to
my childhood experience. Family life had failed me, in a
way, but I had the hospital instead, and college felt familiar
in an institutional sense, with its regular schedule and the
large number of people always in close proximity.

The college had an excellent music school called
Crane and an emphasis on culture which I appreciated. The
entire freshman class had the opportunity to take a class trip
to New York City, where one of the events planned for us
was a rehearsal of the Crane chorus singing under the
direction of the conductor Toscanini – the same composer
whose work I'd become well acquainted with while
listening to the radio on the children's ward at the hospital

in Watertown! I joined a theater club called Black Friars and worked on the technical crew.

At the end of my freshman year I was accepted into a fraternity. This turned out to be not only fun but also useful, because for the remaining years of college I lived in the fraternity house and, when everyone went home for the summer, I could stay on as "House Father." This role required me to look after the frat house and collect a few bucks a week in rent money from each of the students who lived there while going to summer school. (In New York at the time keeping certification as a teacher meant taking summer school courses on a fairly regular basis.) It also enabled me to take summer courses, work on summer theater productions (We did *La Bohème, Oklahoma!,* and *Die Fledermaus* during my three summers. I did stage work, lighting, and makeup), and take on some odd jobs (mostly in the college cafeteria, dishwashing department, though one summer I barhopped for a while).

It was through my House Father position that I acquired my first typewriter. One of the students who had been living in the frat for the summer ended his session unable to pay me the $24 he owed in rent money. He told me in lieu of rent, he could give me a Smith-Corona Standard typewriter which he had liberated from the Army some years before in beautiful working condition. I agreed to the deal and used that typewriter for years. Eventually I passed it along to someone else, but I've often wished I had it back. It was a good reliable machine.

The college was co-ed but the students were strictly segregated. Women had curfews and were required to sign in to their dorms at night. My senior year, the Dean of Men took it upon himself to cleanse the campus of all homosexual influences. Those of us who had not been observed to do a lot of dating, which included me, were called into his office and required to answer questions about our sexual preferences.

One young man he called in as part of this interview process was Charlie, a slender, high-energy music student who was only about five feet tall and known for his love of ballet as well as music. The dean said, "Tell me, Charlie, are you queer?" Charlie opened the door to the dean's office so that the half-dozen or so students waiting in the hall could hear. Then he shouted, "What kind of question is that? Am I *queer*? Do you mean do I fuck *animals*? The answer is no!"

The next morning, signs appeared all over campus that said, "The birdwatchers' club will entertain the Clarkson hockey team tonight in room 205." Well, room

205 happened to be the men's room. More signs appeared, and then there was a new sign that said, "No one may post notices on these boards without permission of the dean." The next morning there was a sign under *that* sign saying, "The dean will not post notices on this board without permission of the birdwatchers' club."

This went on all year, much to the dean's fury. He demanded to know who was posting the signs and ordered all the custodians to keep watch, but the custodians assured him they had seen nothing. Of course we all assumed it was Charlie, and as far as I'm concerned, it was a success – score one for Charlie!

My plan when I started out at college was to become a teacher, but when junior year came along and I had to do some student teaching, I discovered that I wasn't very good at it. I had a work study job at school shelving books in the library, and the librarian who oversaw my work suggested that I apply to the library degree program instead. And I found that was a very good match for me. I took a few courses to make up the requirements I'd need to graduate. I continued my job in the library and was accepted to the master's degree program in library science at Albany State College for the following fall.

~6~

1955-1956: Albany

In September of 1955 I arrived at Albany State College, which is now SUNY Albany, and found a room in a boarding house across from the college. The city was entirely new to me. Albany is the capital of New York state, and at that time there was a general belief that it was being run by a corrupt political machine. Supposedly when elections were being held, people would show up on campus and offer students five dollars each to vote per their instructions.

One thing I remember well about Albany is the women climbing trees with buckets of water to wash the leaves, a tradition that early immigrants brought over from Holland. Another local tradition, popular among the college students, was to buy bread at Freihoffer's Bakery. There was a joke that Freihoffer's had a contract for their horses to fill the potholes in the streets.

The library science program was rigorous, but I found it fascinating. We had a teacher named Carolyn Howard, tall and thin with marcel finger waves, whose main interest was what we called kiddie lit. She introduced me to *The Hobbit* just as the entire *Lord of the Rings* trilogy was being published in the U.S. for the first time. I loved *The Hobbit* and was grateful to Miss Howard for exposing me to the book.

One day in class we asked her why she became a librarian. She told us that growing up, she was tall for her age, and when she was fourteen years old her father called her into his office, sat her down opposite his desk, and said, "We have to face the fact that you're not an attractive woman and you will not get a good husband, so your mother and I have decided you will become a librarian so that you can support yourself."

In addition to literature, we studied cataloguing, something I turned out to have a talent for. The program was one year long and attracted a variety of students. One was a Catholic priest who had been working in the bishop's headquarters in Albany when the bishop called him in and said, "I need a librarian to manage my library, so you will go to Albany State to become a librarian. Thank you, you are excused now." I asked the priest if he felt like it was his choice. He said that if he didn't agree with the order he would instead be sent to Congo as a missionary, so he was glad to be there.

Life at the boarding house was quiet and routine. I'd eat breakfast there in the morning, go to school for the day, and come back at night. I got to know another resident who was working at a laboratory in a government facility that was designing rocket engines and jet engines. This was the beginning of the space age.

When I had breaks from school, I took the train home to see my family. By that time, my brother Norman was a married farmer; David was in the Army; and Howard and Betty were still in school. My father, in what we had no way of knowing was the last year of his life, was still his carefree self, mainly interested in hunting and fishing, and not always paying much attention to the other details of life. Years after my grandmother died, my uncle pointed out that my father had never bothered to pay property taxes, and whenever the government threatened to charge him with tax evasion, my grandmother would pay up. So technically she owned my parents' house all that time.

~7~

1956-1960: Cortland

I completed my master's degree in spring of 1956 and accepted a position in technical services at SUNY Cortland's library. My role was to order and catalogue books; student workers did the shelving. It was a good job for me. The only drawback was that I sometimes became engrossed in the books and fell behind on cataloguing! There were so many topics that interested me – history, religion, poetry, science, sometimes even fiction. I spent far more time reading on the job than I should have.

I was not much of a churchgoer in those days. One of my new colleagues at the library persuaded me to join him and his family for a Sunday service at the Methodist church, but it didn't really interest me. Then the college registrar suggested that I try *his* church, which was Universalist, and I agreed to go.

The Universalist minister's name was Max Coots, and he started the sermon with a poem that went, "Praise God from whom all cyclones blow, praise him when rivers overflow, praise God ye heavenly host, when people drown and children roast." That perked my ears up! Suddenly I was interested in this church. It was within walking distance of the downtown Cortland's YMCA, where I was renting a room, and I began attending regularly. And I was still within walking distance later that year, when I moved to an apartment in the back of a house across the street from the Y.

I'd always enjoyed going to church; I just couldn't abide the strict Mennonite theology with which I was raised. The Universalist church offered me a place where I could believe what I chose rather than what I was told to believe. I'd never even heard of Universalism before, but I was drawn in immediately.

The year I began attending Cortland's Universalist parish was Max Coots' last year as minister. He moved on to a position in Canton, New York, where he would spend the remainder of his career. In the fall a new minister named Jim Hunt arrived to replace him.

Jim wrote his sermons on Saturdays. One Sunday he seemed to be talking on and on and on, as the congregation grew increasingly restless. After the service ended, I said to him, "Jim, that was an awfully long sermon!"

Jim told me, "When I sit down to write a sermon, I put five sheets of paper on my desk, set my typewriter on double-space and type until I come to the end of the fifth sheet. Yesterday I forgot to set my typewriter on double-space."

I considered Jim a terrific minister, but I think the rest of the congregation found him a bit too politically radical. His desk was a wooden door that said "Men." I asked him where he got it. He said that it was from a police station in Syracuse where he had once spent the night after getting arrested for protesting an urban renewal project, what they used to call Negro removal, which consisted of tearing down the structures in the parts of town where black people lived and building high-rises in their place. Later, the police station itself was torn down, and the pieces were sold off. Jim bought the men's room door as a souvenir of the protest and his arrest.

Jim didn't stay long at our church, deciding soon that he wanted to earn a doctoral degree at Syracuse University, after which he taught in Raleigh, North Carolina. He was a scholar of Gandhi, writing books about him and spending long periods of time in India and South Africa researching his life. When Jim shared the news that he was leaving our church, he urged me to consider a career in ministry.

I had become increasingly involved in church life during that year, and I'd met my future wife. Trudi was a young childless widow who was living with her sister, also a widow, and helping her sister to raise her four children. But Trudi was ready to move away from her sister and was looking for a place to live, so Jim Hunt's wife Jane suggested she ask me if I had any leads. I didn't, but I offered to look at apartments with her. We started spending a lot of time together, visiting various properties and talking about furnishings and so forth, and with some matchmaking pressure from Jane, it soon turned into a romantic relationship.

Trudi was six years my senior, a farmgirl from Auburn, New York. One of her brothers had been an Air Force mechanic stationed in England during World War II. She had been married to a pilot who flew light planes and helicopters and did patrol work in Korea. The day after the armistice was signed ending the Korean War, he was called into service on a helicopter patrol to cover for a pilot who was sick. Over the ocean off the coast of Japan, the helicopter experienced mechanical failure and crashed. He was sent home in a sealed coffin; she was never allowed to see the body.

That was in 1955, two years before we met. Had her husband been killed one day earlier, before the armistice, she would have been eligible for far more benefits. But she needed to support herself, so she attended business school and learned bookkeeping, which it turned out she had a terrific talent for. She could pick up a sheet of paper with numbers on it and say right away that the figures didn't add up. Then she'd sit down with her adding machine until she'd found the problem.

Prior to meeting Trudi, I had assumed I'd never get married. I never dated. My plans were to spend the rest of my life as a librarian, cataloguing books. I believed myself to be so physically compromised after all those years in the hospital, and somewhere I picked up the message that I wasn't likely to live very long into adulthood. Having met patients in the hospital who were having their second or third bout of tuberculosis, I knew I was a candidate for recurrence. Not until many years later, after we had settled in Carlisle, did a doctor put me on a year's worth of antibiotics to eradicate any last trace of the Tb strain.

But then I met Trudi and we hit it off. And Trudi agreed with our minister, Jim Hunt, that I should consider theological school. We were talking about marriage, and as she saw it, my being a minister would afford us a much more interesting future than my being a librarian would. She wanted more from life than looking at books. One Sunday Bob Cope, then at St. Lawrence, gave a sermon on the school and the students studying for the ministry. As to why people went into the liberal ministry, he told us, it was because they were seeking help for their loneliness, both cosmic and personal – seeking salvation, I believe was his expression. Coming on top of Jim Hunt's encouragement and Trudi's urging, it was enough to convince me. So I applied to theological school.

Trudi and I got married on May 7, 1960 at the Cortland Universalist church where we met, with a reception afterwards in the basement. The celebration was low-key but fun and festive. My father was gone by then, but my mother and other family members attended, as did Trudi's mother, sister and relatives.

Trudi knew a couple who lived on a large farm in Pennsylvania owned by a member of the Dupont family, managing their herd of golden Guernseys. For our honeymoon, we drove to Pennsylvania and stayed with them for a few days. One morning while we were there, we were eating breakfast when our host came in from the barn and said that a cow was in labor but things weren't going well and we would need to help. I said I didn't know how to deliver a calf, but he said all I'd have to do was pull!

So I went out with him and did just what he told me to do. He'd managed to hook a chain around the calf's legs and gave me the end of the chain to pull. Eventually it worked, and the calf slid on out! It was a messy job; I had to wash all my clothes and take a shower, but the sense of accomplishment was terrific. After that I always liked to say that one of my major accomplishments in life was that I had helped to deliver a calf. I don't know whether it was indeed as significant as I liked to make it out to be, but in fact we had saved a life and done a good deed, so it really was an accomplishment of sorts.

~8~

1960-1963: Crane Theological School

I'd been accepted at two theological schools: St. Lawrence and Crane, which was part of Tufts University. I asked our minister in Cortland, Jim Hunt, which one he thought I should choose. He observed that I'd spent my whole life living in rural settings and it would probably be good for me to get a taste of city living, so I should go to Crane. I took his advice and enrolled in the three-year Bachelor of Divinity program there.

We arrived in Medford, Massachusetts in the fall of 1960 and found an apartment on the top floor of a house that was within walking distance of the Tufts campus. Shortly after we arrived, Trudi started a job in the billing department at Beacon Press, the publishing house of the American Unitarian Association. She commuted into Boston every day on the subway. Beacon Press had lots of unpaid bills for Trudi to sort out, since ministers were notorious for charging books and then not paying for them.

Trudi and I joined a church in Medford, but we didn't attend every Sunday. We were both working hard all week and sometimes we just wanted Sundays off. Our apartment turned out not to be a great find because the lights kept popping out and one day the landlord told me he had finally fixed all the fuses. I asked him how. He said a friend had told him if you just stick a penny under the fuse as you screwed it in, the fuse wouldn't blow. Although he was right, I knew that this was also a major fire hazard. So I told Trudi I thought we'd better move.

I asked our minister in Medford, Gene Adams, if he knew of any available housing. He introduced me to a woman in the congregation who owned a house that she soon planned to sell, and she agreed that we could rent rooms in it from her. It was located on the back side of the Tufts campus and an easy walk to classes for me. Trudi opted to find a job closer to home so that she wouldn't have to commute into Boston and was hired by the Tufts business office.

The next two years were very pleasant for both of us. I enjoyed all of my classes at Crane. As a liberal theological school, it attracted mostly Unitarians and Universalists. I entered as a Universalist, although my first year of divinity school saw the merging of the Unitarians and Universalists into what is now the Unitarian Universalist faith. I never shed my belief that Universalism was the better of the two!

Very early in my theological studies, I felt certain that I had found my calling. I was fascinated by all that we were learning and discussing, but especially humanism, which was rapidly growing in popularity in Unitarian Universalist circles. Essentially that means religion without God, and it's what both of the ministers who had had so much influence over me in Cortland and led me into the ministry – Max Coots and Jim Hunt – followed.

It was during that time, while walking across the Tufts campus, that I had the first of what I would describe as a full-blown mystical experience: hard to put into words, but I had the sensation that the physical world became entirely transparent and I was walking on nothing. I had the sensation that I was being flooded with knowledge and I had no reason to wonder or doubt about anything. It was a real high. I had no sense of time while experiencing it, but I'm certain it didn't last very long.

My classmates at Crane and I all started searching for ministries as we approached completion of our degree program in spring of 1963. I considered a position in Outlaws Bridge, North Carolina, but my visit there coincided with the great civil rights march in Washington, D.C., and I simply didn't believe that I was prepared to manage all of the issues that were sure to be facing a Southern church as issues of civil rights burgeoned. I didn't feel experienced enough to meet the needs of this congregation. So instead I found an opportunity in Stafford, Connecticut, that seemed like a better match for me, and Trudi and I began preparing to leave Massachusetts for Connecticut.

~*9*~

1963-1969: Stafford and Laconia

Stafford was a nearly defunct mill town. Earlier it had contained a textile mill, a button mill and a woolen mill. When we arrived it had one mill still manufacturing material for military uniforms, but the contract with the Navy was nearing its end and then there would be no functioning mills at all – just lots of great big empty brick buildings.

The church at the time we arrived was struggling, with about thirty people regularly attending Sunday services and an entrenched leadership that consisted of a very small number of families who did not want anything about the church to change and did not want anyone else to help run it. For staff, there was a high school girl who played the organ and a custodian who cleaned the building, and that was about it. I ran off the orders of service every week on a mimeograph machine.

The church treasurer was the president of the Stafford Springs Bank. The report he submitted for annual meeting said, "We have enough money to run the church." I asked how much that was. He answered, "Enough." No one had any idea what our bank balance was because the treasurer saw no reason to share that information. His attitude toward me was that the leadership had things entirely under control and my role was to deliver sermons and not ask questions.

Trudi and I moved into the parsonage, a big old house build in the late 1800s onto which a large wing had been added to host the church's social functions. Back in the heyday of the town's mills there had probably been a lot of church events, but when I arrived there were so few that the function space was rented out to a preschool. Every morning while I worked, I could hear the children singing "Good morning to you! Good morning to you!"

The parishioners had mixed reactions to me, to say the least. There was one gentleman who wore eyeglasses with hearing aids built into the earpieces. From the pulpit, after we'd sung the opening hymn and I'd offered words of greeting, I'd see him take off his glasses and put them in his pocket, and I knew that meant he never heard a single

word of my sermon. Then he'd put his glasses back on –
and his hearing aids back in – for the final hymn.

Trudi and I expected to stay there for more than just
a year, but once we were settled in we did not feel that the
church leadership treated us very well. They had a lot of
criticisms of how I did things, and they didn't like my
politics: they were Goldwater followers whereas I
supported Johnson. When President Kennedy was
assassinated it barely made a ripple in my congregation
compared with many other places. The congregation didn't
support Kennedy anyway. For many of my peers, the
assassination was a flashpoint for their ministries, but in
Stafford, Connecticut, not much was required of me at all
in the context of that national crisis.

Bad feelings grew until Trudi declared that she was
not going to attend church anymore. She was terrifically
supportive of my career, but she could no longer abide the
animosity in the Stafford church. Once she said that, I
realized there was no point in our staying. So I let the UUA
know that I was looking for a new posting, and I resigned.

The UUA sent me to Laconia, New Hampshire. My
reception there was much warmer than in Stafford.
Although my role was supposed to be interim minister –
which is a minister who fills in temporarily while the

church is searching for a permanent hire – after two months they had decided that I should stay.

We were happy at the Unitarian Universalist Church of Laconia from the beginning. The church was small and picturesque, on the shores of Lake Winnipesaukee. It was the only church I've worked for that didn't close during the summer, as was the common practice at the time. Laconia is a summer vacation community and our attendance actually grew when all the snowbirds came back north from Florida! We typically had about thirty people in the regular year, and forty or fifty in the summer. The congregation was made up of very nice people with whom we got along easily. We had a good organist and a talented choir.

I enjoyed getting to know the members of the congregation. There was a woman who sold antiques, and I still own a couple of the items we bought from her. There was a man who had previously worked for the printing office at the U.S. Treasury. He made friends with the custodian who emptied the wastebaskets, and the custodian would save him the irregular sheets of stamps that were deemed not usable and were to be destroyed. He built a collection of stamps deemed unusable because their color was slightly off; I'm guessing that collection would be worth a fortune. Stamp collectors love things like that! He was politically conservative, a right-wing Republican who thought the election of FDR was the worst thing to ever happen to the country, but we managed, just barely, to get along. It was a source of pride to him that his wife had been in the Red Cross and enforced a rule that blood donated by African-Americans had to be clearly labeled so it wouldn't be given to white soldiers.

Through some members of the congregation, Trudi found an office job with an attorney who counted among his clients Grace Metalious, the author of *Peyton Place.* Because she was the target of so many libel and defamation suits by readers who claimed they were clearly identifiable among her characters, the attorney had required her to sit in his office and write her autobiography so that he could better defend her. They kept the autobiography in a safe. Grace Metalious died before Trudi arrived, and the attorney is long gone as well. I sometimes wonder what happened to the autobiography that lay in their safe.

Having settled comfortably into the parsonage and decided we wanted to stay in Laconia, we set about starting a family. Because of surgery Trudi had undergone when she was younger, we knew all along that we couldn't have biological children, and so we initiated the adoption process. We established a relationship with an agency and started working with a social worker, who interviewed us to establish our credibility and character and determined that we were capable of nurturing a family.

Our son Nathan was sixteen months old when he was given to us in 1966, and we were provided almost no information about his background or infancy. But every now and then, we'd get glimmers of hints. One day a high school girl from the congregation said she wanted to play us an album she'd just bought. It was "Sergeant Pepper's Lonely Hearts Club Band," and the moment the music started, Nathan looked up from where he was playing and then collapsed on the floor, crying uncontrollably. So that made us think someone in his foster home had played the Beatles. It was just such an indelible image, the way he sobbed and sobbed the moment he heard the music. And whenever he heard a dog bark outside, he'd run to the window to see it, which gave us the idea that they had had a dog. But for the most part, everything about his past was kept strictly secret from us.

Once Nathan had settled into our household and we were comfortable in our role as parents, Trudi expressed to the adoption agency that she'd like a daughter as well. The following year, in 1967, we received a somewhat mysterious phone call from the social worker, saying, "We have a twelve-week-old girl here....*if* you'd like her."

We didn't understand. Of course we would like a baby girl – we'd already made that clear. What was the problem?

"What do you mean, '*If* we'd like her?'" Trudi asked.

The social worker explained that the infant was part American Indian and that the state board that handled adoption cases believed it would be impossible to find an adoptive home for her because of that. The state was pressuring the agency to put the baby in an orphanage. Trudi and I were shocked and said we didn't care a bit about her ethnicity; we just wanted a daughter!

We eventually found out that our daughter Nancie's biological father had been a Sioux Indian. My granddaughter Stefanie – Nancie's daughter – and I share a theory that one of her ancestors was responsible for scalping General Custer at Little Big Horn. In any case, Nancie receives a $10 check from the government every year for royalties on the oil wells located on Sioux lands.

During my time as minister in Laconia, the UUA asked me to sit on the board of the New Hampshire Council of Churches. The chair of that board was a Baptist minister, but he was very accepting of the diversity of religions represented on that board. He understood that it was in the board's best interest for all of us to work together. The board's purpose was to unite churches over common issues, and the critical issue we faced in the late 1960s was civil rights, so that was something we spent a lot of time considering. We discussed race relations, prejudice, systems for racial integration. That was over fifty years ago now, and the world has changed a lot in that regard, though unfortunately not as much as we hoped at the time it would.

The Laconia church was where I first went through many of the experiences beyond Sunday sermons that make up a minister's career. When it came to pastoral care, I relied heavily on Trudi's support. She was always a tremendous source of strength in that regard. I really do believe that ninety percent of pastoral care when someone is grieving is showing up. What can you say or do to someone experiencing loss other than just be present with them? You learn as you go. And sometimes you make mistakes – I made some terrible mistakes – but you learn from your mistakes. It's a gradual process. But again, you show up for people, and the fact that you are willing to be with them is a start.

Funerals and memorial services were more standardized back then than they are now. We didn't have websites to refer to, but we had books and pamphlets, and we ministers drew upon one another for help. We almost always did the 23rd Psalm for a funeral service – *The Lord is my shepherd; I shall not want. He maketh me to lie down in green pastures: he leadeth me beside the still waters. He restoreth my soul* – and the Lord's Prayer. Now, all of that is far less common in UU memorial services or funerals. People say to me, "None of that, we don't want that kind of stuff. We want everything to be different." Services today are less about ritualistic text and more about how the individual being memorialized will be missed.

When the church gave me time off in the summer, we'd visit friends who owned a place in Green River, Vermont. We liked the area so much that we bought a cabin up the road from our friends. They had children just a little bit older than ours, and it was always a pleasure in the summer for our families to spend time together. We'd travel to New York in the summer as well. Trudi's family had an annual reunion in Auburn, and while we were in the area we'd visit my family also. We wanted our children to know their relatives. I never did feel close to my family. Trudi was more of a family person. She liked to visit all of them, and she enjoyed having her mother come stay with us in Laconia.

My faith was what was then considered humanism. I was a humanist, but not all of my congregants were, so I had to be cautious not to force those beliefs on people. The belief was that to be a humanist was to reject Christianity and all that went with it. I remember the dean at Crane Theological School remarking that he was overwhelmed by what he saw as weird people whom he was trying to train to be ministers despite the fact that they didn't like to pray. At that time we thought humanism was the wave of the future. Maybe so – for about two years!

In any case, with my congregation in Laconia I had to restrain my humanist tendencies. It wasn't what they'd grown up with or what they believed. I had to draw upon the Bible and the old red hymn book that UU churches used back then, which was much more traditional than what we have now. That hymnal had all the traditional words for the hymns. Now UUs like to change all of the words so it's not too Godly or Christian, and sometimes I wonder why. I had a friend in theological school who suggested we keep all the hymns in Latin, so that we could sing them without arguing about the words.

Our tenure in Laconia came to an end when a
parishioner – I think the politically conservative one whose
wife had been a Red Cross nurse – started a petition to fire
me. The congregation held a meeting, the petition was
rejected, and I was told that therefore I could stay, but
knowing there was active opposition to my presence, Trudi
and I felt that it was time for us to leave and find a new
church.

In those days, ministers didn't think in terms of
ascending a career ladder; you just made lateral moves
from one church to another at essentially the same salary. I
paid a visit to the UUA headquarters in Boston to ask to be
put into the candidate pool for the upcoming year, but there
wasn't much available at the time.

I returned to the UUA headquarters another day for
a meeting with the placement staff and one of the people in
that department said, "Hey, I'll tell you what. There's a
church in Cape Town, South Africa, that's looking for a
minister!"

I said, "*Cape Town?* You've got to be kidding."

He said, "Go home and think about it," and gave me
some material.

I went home and Trudi asked me how my meeting had gone. I said, "He asked me if I'd consider South Africa. I said no!"

Trudi said, "Woody, you're a stick in the mud! Go back and tell him you're interested!" So I did as she said. And I was offered the position.

~10~

1969-1972: Cape Town

Once again, Trudi had changed the course of my life, as she so often did. Were it not for her, I would have remained a librarian forever. I was content enough cataloguing books, but I wouldn't say I was happy with that life. Trudi's insistence that I apply to theological school gave me a career that brought me happiness. And Trudi's insistence that I consider the position in South Africa brought the two of us an opportunity I never would have even considered had she not spoken up.

The founding minister of the Unitarian church in South Africa was a man named David Pieter Faure, born in Cape Province, South Africa in 1842. Raised in the Dutch Reform church, he studied theology at the University of Leiden. One day the dean summoned Faure to his office and said, "You're from South Africa. Do you speak English?" Faure said that he was bilingual, speaking both Dutch and English. The dean said, "There's this peculiar thing going on in the U.S. with a fellow named Theodore Parker and someone else named Ellery Channing. We have their books, but no one here reads English." He gave Faure the books and asked him to read them.

Faure read them, and the ideas of Parker and Channing resonated with him so powerfully that he gave a sermon after his return to Cape Town on their teachings at a Dutch Reform church, after which he was told that those ideas were not acceptable in the Dutch Reform faith. So in 1867 he founded the nation's first Unitarian church.

In 1910, after two centuries of Dutch and British colonization, an act of the British Parliament granted nominal independence by creating the Union of South Africa out of former territories of the Cape, Transvaal and Natal colonies, as well as the Orange Free State republic. At the time, nonwhites were allowed to vote in Cape Town, where voting rights were determined by property ownership, but not elsewhere in the new nation. Faure set about lobbying for the rights of nonwhite people. When a heckler questioned his loyalties, he said, "The vote is not a question of race; it's a question of justice. And I love justice more than race." Unfortunately, his crusade was unsuccessful, and nonwhites outside of Cape Town were not allowed to register to vote until 1994.

The decision having been made that Trudi and I would relocate our family to South Africa, I set about procuring the necessary visa. I applied by mail to the South African embassy in Washington, D.C. I waited and waited for a response to my visa application. By then I'd resigned from the Laconia church and the four of us had moved temporarily to Brattleboro, Vermont, where we were staying in the home of a minister friend.

I sent the embassy letters and I made phone calls, inquiring as to the status of my visa. Again and again I was told that it was in progress. While we waited for instructions, I read books on South Africa. Finally, a newspaper reporter in Cape Town named Bob Steyne who was a member of the Unitarian church there and knew about the delay ran into the Minister of the Interior and asked him to facilitate the process. Next I received a letter asking about my position on race relations. I tried to answer tactfully.

A couple of weeks later I got a phone call. It was the South African ambassador calling from D.C. to apologize for the slow processing of my visa and reassuring me that it was on its way. Later I asked Bob Steyne what had gotten the process moving along. He said that the Minister of the Interior had personally insisted on it.

After we'd settled in Cape Town, I got to know Bob Steyne a little bit better. He was an Afrikaaner and had been covering a local meeting for the Cape Argus Newspaper, a liberal English language newspaper, when a brief discussion arose about the church. Someone remarked, "You might as well be a communist as be a Unitarian."

That statement caught Bob's attention and he decided to go check out this controversial church. There he found an American minister named Victor Carpenter preaching. Bob liked what he heard and stayed with the church. Coincidentally enough, nearly forty years later, that same Victor Carpenter would serve as interim minister in Carlisle after I retired while the congregation searched for a permanent replacement. Eventually Bob Steyne became ordained as a minister himself.

With the visa cleared and the church in Cape Town awaiting our arrival, Trudi and I along with our two very young children left the U.S. in October of 1969 and flew to London. We stayed near Tavistock Square, which had once been home to Virginia Woolf. The block of houses where she had lived was bombed during the war and replaced by a hotel. In the center of the square was a park that featured a statue of Gandhi. We loved London and we especially loved that statue. We returned to the city several more times in the decades that followed, and we always stayed in that same area so that we could spend time with Gandhi.

We remained in London for a week. I attended meetings with the staff of the British General Assembly of Free Protestant and Unitarian Churches, during which I learned more about Cape Town and the church there, but we also had plenty of time to explore London. We even fit in a trip to Stonehenge. At the time it was unfenced, so we could walk around examining the carvings and rubbing our hands on the stones, which is probably why now it is surrounded by fencing.

When the week was up, we flew from London to Johannesburg, where members of the local Unitarian church met us and escorted us to the flight that would take us to Cape Town. In Cape Town, we were met by parishioners who welcomed us and drove us to the parsonage – our new home.

The parsonage was located in a suburban section of Cape Town called Vredehoek, which had pretty houses with red tiled roofs. One thing we noticed right away was that there were no screens in any windows, because there were so few insects in Cape Town. Since South Africa is in the Southern Hemisphere, when we arrived in October it was spring. The wind blows there constantly; all the trees we saw leaned one way because of it, and the wind was also the reason for the lack of flying insects.

We were impressed right away with the parsonage, a large house at the foot of Table Mountain. Our bedroom had a big bay window overlooking the harbor, and there were bedrooms for each of the children. The kitchen had a warming plate drawer in the bottom of the stove; it was considered uncivilized to eat off an unwarmed plate. We had a washing machine but no dryer; there was a clothesline in the backyard, and clothes dried quickly in the warm wind. There was a maid's room which had been converted into an office supply room for the church. The backyard was stepped into several levels. There were fig trees, apple trees, an avocado tree and an almond tree. There was also a shed which had previously been used as servants' quarters.

For several weeks, the parsonage lacked linens, dishes and small appliances. We had been told that it was a better idea to ship our household goods from the U.S. rather than buy items in South Africa, but the longshoremen had gone on strike, and so we had to wait for our belongings. One of the parishioners who ran a laundry supplied us with sheets, pillowcases and towels until ours arrived.

The church itself was located downtown in a former warehouse. It was a big building guarded by a large iron gate. The pulpit was high up and the congregants sat in folding chairs. In conducting weddings, I was serving as an official of the government. And so I had to pass a test to be allowed to officiate over weddings. One of the questions was whether it was legal to marry people of different races. Of course I was well aware that in South Africa, the correct answer to that question was no.

As we acquainted ourselves with our new environment, we made diverse and interesting friends. One was Mr. Ibraham, who delivered fresh produce to our door. He was Muslim and drove around in a pickup truck loaded with fruits and vegetables. He also owned a store located in District Six, the so-called "coloured district." He and his wife invited us to their home for dinner, and we learned their custom of eating with our fingers. One evening we were talking about money, and I admitted I'd forgotten what American currency looked like. Mr. Ibraham reached into his pocket and pulled out a roll of American twenties. I asked where he had gotten them. He said that young women brought them into the store, having gotten them from American sailors. I didn't ask any further questions, because I was fairly sure he was talking about something not terribly legal!

What the apartheid system in South Africa essentially meant was that the government was in the business of defining races – of which there were many. Even though movie theaters, restaurants, schools and other public places were strictly segregated, the government did not impose segregation on churches. I think this was at the insistence of the Dutch Reform Church, which was South Africa's principal white religion.

As a result, our Unitarian congregation included several "coloured," as they were designated there. One of them worked for a company that manufactured coffins. He invited me to tea one afternoon. I discovered that he lived in a beautiful part of the city that looked like New Orleans, with wrought iron balconies and fancy painted houses. I made my way to the address I'd been given and discovered that the coffin factory was a big open plot with a tin roof over it. The man introduced me to his boss and said that we were all going to have tea together. We pulled up chairs around an unfinished coffin, and that served as our table. I really enjoyed that visit.

There was another so-called coloured who worked as a tailor, making suits, coats and other apparel for women. He was able to buy an empty lot and build a house for his family. Then the National Party took over and started dividing Cape Town into white and nonwhite – or "Nie Blanke," in Afrikaans. The area where the man's house was located was designated a white section. He was told he could stay there as long as he wanted, but once he left – whether through death or by selling the house – the next owner would have to be white.

He soon realized that this meant if he died, his wife and children would not be allowed to keep the house. And so he sold it, not wanting at all to leave but feeling compelled to protect the future interests of his family. Had he not done so, they could have been thrown out on the street in his absence. It was a terrible way for the government to treat people.

The church gave us a loan to buy a car. My initial impression was that we'd been sold a dud, because every time I pushed the gas pedal down, the car started to choke. I told my friend Bob Steyne, the newspaper reporter who had helped facilitate my visa, that I thought I'd gotten taken on the car deal. He asked what was wrong. I described the way the car coughed and sputtered and didn't have any pickup. He asked what kind of gas I was using. I said regular. He told me I should be using high-test. I said, "But why wouldn't the guy at the filling station tell me that?"

Bob asked what color the filling station attendant was. I said he was Bantu, meaning black. Bob said, "As a nonwhite person in South Africa, he is allowed only to take orders. If you've been telling him to use regular, that's what he would do. If you told him to pee in the gas tank, he'd do that. He has no choice."

So the next time I stopped at the gas station, I asked the attendant to fill it. He said, "With what?" I said, "What *should* I be using?" He said, "This car needs high-test." I said, "Fill it with high-test then."

And from then on the car ran beautifully. I thought, "What kind of an insane political system are we living under here, when a guy like me can tell you to do something stupid and because of your skin color and his, you can't correct him?" After that, each time I went to the gas station, we'd go through the same ritual: I'd say "Fill it please." He'd say, "With what?" I'd say, "With high-test." And he'd say, "Yes boss." It was just a small sign of how crazy the system was.

When Nathan was old enough for kindergarten, we enrolled him in the Faure School for Boys, presumably named after a relative of the minister who started our church. Like all the students there, Nathan wore a red and white checked shirt, a red jacket with an owl insignia on the pocket, shorts and a little red beanie. During his two years at the school he learned some Afrikaans.

Both of our children would play with the other kids in the neighborhood. Two houses up from us was a physician whose maid had a son close in age to our kids. He'd come play with them, always carrying a tin plate that he used as a steering wheel because he pretended he was a bus driver. We learned one Afrikaans phrase: *"Moinie met klippe hoi nei"* – "Do not throw stones" –except in Afrikaans you use a double-negative so to us it seemed more like we were saying "Do not with little stones throw not." The first time Trudi yelled that, the little boy was so surprised he almost fell over.

The Cape Town church was a lovely place for me to minister for so many reasons. We had a wonderful organist from Cape Town University named David Oliver. He knew a wide range of musicians in the region, so we often had excellent soloists and other talented instrumentalists. One day David told me that he was planning a party at his home and would like to invite Trudi and me but wanted to know first if I thought Trudi would be comfortable with gay people, because a lot of the guests would be gay. I said I did not think that would be a problem for Trudi! We went and had a good time, and were happy to get to know members of Cape Town's gay community better during our remaining time in South Africa.

Trudi did a lot of social activities with our church friends when she wasn't busy caring for the children. She formed a fast friendship with David Oliver's partner, John de Beer. Once a week the maid who cleaned the church would come to clean the parsonage. She didn't mind babysitting for the children while she was there, so Trudi would go to the movies with John. David and John and the Steynes were our closest friends in those years.

We visited Johannesburg during our stay in South Africa but didn't venture much farther than that because most of the countries surrounding us were engaged in civil wars and so it wasn't really safe to travel. Rhodesia had recently declared its independence from Britain but was resisting the push to integrate and had sealed most of its borders. We did occasionally have visitors from Rhodesia, and we had a babysitter from there who was attending Cape Town University.

South Africa continued to have its own racial problems, of course. The police treated nonwhites so harshly that even white people would hesitate to report a petty crime because the police response would be so disproportionate to the crime. If someone pilfered something from your home or your shop, you'd let it go rather than report it to the police because you didn't want to witness a police beating.

We had a portable radio in our kitchen which I hung over a door handle. We'd listen to music, and every day at noon there was a broadcast of a reading from the series *The Durrells in Corfu* by Gerald Durrell; at other times we'd listen to music. One day the delivery boy who worked for our fruit and vegetable man came in for his usual payment. He dropped off our order and then left. A few minutes later the fruit and vegetable man came to the door asking for his delivery boy. I said he'd already left.

"That means he's run off with my money," the vendor said. Then I looked at the door and saw that the radio was gone as well.

I said, "I suppose I should call the police."

The vendor said, "You could, but I wish you'd let me handle it myself. He's a street urchin. I can find him." That solution was fine with me, given what I knew of the police and how they were likely to treat the boy for this petty theft.

At that time in South Africa there were fourteen different classifications of race, and you can imagine the divisiveness that this caused. For example, we had an older church member who was the retired principal of a teacher training college. After I arrived, he stopped attending church. I paid him a visit to try to find out if I had offended or annoyed him.

He said that because of his failing eyesight, he had to take a city bus to church, and for many years he had endured the necessity of riding in the back of the bus, but under the apartheid system his bus line had been entirely segregated. So he'd stand on the corner waiting to catch the bus to church, and he'd watch two or three buses designated for white people pass by without stopping, each with four or five people in them. Then the bus he was allowed to use – the nonwhite, or "nie Blanke" in the Afrikaaner language, bus – would come along usually late and very crowded. He'd have to pack himself into to this overcrowded bus having just seen several empty buses pass by. He told me he loved the church but he had his dignity, and this situation was just too much for him.

Since he would not attend church, I made the trip out to visit him at home a few more times and learned a bit about his background. He had a son who had graduated from Cape Town University, which did not ordinarily take nonwhite students but had taken him to study physics, there being no "coloured" colleges offering that major. Upon graduation he was offered a scholarship to do a Ph.D. program at MIT, based on the recommendations of the faculty at Cape Town University. When he went to the passport bureau to apply for his passport and told the official that he was going to do graduate work at MIT, the official said, "You are wasting your time. We don't need any coloured physicists in South Africa." The young man said he wanted to go anyway. The official said he would provide an exit visa but no return visa, meaning that the young man might never be allowed back into South Africa. And the young man took that deal and left the country.

Two years later, the same couple's daughter was in nearly the same situation. She had graduated from medical school and opened an office in the coloured district of Cape Town. One of her patients had to be hospitalized. Coloured doctors were not allowed to care for their own patients in the segregated hospital. She went straight to the Canadian Embassy and inquired as to whether Canada needed any doctors. She was told that they did. She applied for a visa to go work in Canada, and like her brother was granted only an exit visa with no option to return. So this nice old couple watched both of their children leave for North America, never to be allowed back in. Apartheid made for a thoroughly ugly situation throughout the country of South Africa.

The racial problem was just generally inescapable, and so troubling. In our congregation was a wealthy white woman who had a large house and a lot of domestic help. One day the woman and her maid wanted to go shopping downtown. When the taxi she'd called arrived, the driver said he couldn't take the maid because it was a white taxi. So she called a so-called coloured taxi, and that driver arrived and said he couldn't take her because she was white.

This particular conflict rose all the way to Parliament, where the political leaders had to try to figure out what to do about this seemingly irresolvable problem of a white woman who couldn't go shopping with her black maid because of taxi segregation. The solution that Parliament came up with was that they could travel together but it would have to be in a coloured taxi so that the maid didn't contaminate a white taxi. What was even worse was the time that an ambulance was called to the scene of an accident and then the paramedics refused to take the victim because he was coloured. A police officer on the scene finally ordered them to do it anyway. The situation was insane.

And yet despite this despicable racial strife, life was very pleasant there for us. The people in our congregation were lovely. The weather was nice. We'd go for mountainside picnics overlooking the harbor, which is truly the most beautiful cape in the world. I was invited to write a weekly column in Bob Steyne's newspaper for a while. I attended meetings of the interchurch council, which gathered every couple of months at a Quaker meetinghouse. But you could also argue that how effective I was as a minister was demonstrated by the fact that the government never tried to get rid of me. Anyone who was truly and effectively working toward change was soon pushed out.

The part that bothered me most about living in an apartheid state was how it started to seem normal. I became accustomed to taking certain buses and not others, waiting for a white bus if a coloured bus showed up first. I always sensed that the entire population was made up of nice, reasonable people. They were just caught up in a crazy and ridiculous system of segregation. One day Bob Steyne and I drove past a construction site on the highway. I saw black people welding and said to Bob, "I thought certain job skills were restricted, but that site has black welders."

Bob said, "They're not welders; they are welders' *assistants*."

Well, I saw one white man, who was apparently the welder, and fifty black guys who were supposedly the assistants doing all the work. At the post office, too, there were separate lines for whites and nonwhites. But not in the bank. One day I arrived at the bank at the same time as a large African man in greasy overalls with a Mercedes Benz logo. He stepped back to let me go first, but I insisted that he had been there before me and he should go first. He thanked me, and when he reached the window, he pulled from his pocket a zipper envelope that contained the largest amount of cash I'd ever seen in one place in my life. It was probably more than my yearly salary. I thought, "No wonder the bank doesn't care about segregating its customers!"

I think Cape Town helped de-inculturate me. Preparing Christmas services for the beginning of summer and Easter services for the beginning of autumn forced me to throw out all the clichés about the return of the light and the flowers that bloom in the spring. Thanksgiving was not observed, though the English have the remnants of a

Harvest Home celebration, and a whole new history had to be learned and new ways of doing even the commonest things (light switches go down to turn on). South Africans would quiz us about the Vietnam war and seemed unable to comprehend why any country would bog itself down in an endless guerilla war (similar in many ways to the guerilla wars being fought in Angola, Mozambique, and Rhodesia at the time).

I also learned that life is not as simple as we sometimes hope it to be – among the best troops the White Rhodesian Government had were those formerly organized by the Colonial Government as the Rhodesian African Rifles. They remained effective and loyal to the White Government during the entire war.

And my form of happy liberalism didn't necessarily work either. An in-law of the Ibrahims took me aside once at a dinner party and informed me in no uncertain terms that he did not appreciate whites hanging around Coloureds, even if they were Americans. I should stay with my own kind, no matter how nice we were.

I had to acknowledge that the optimistic Humanism of the era had little to offer people living under a repressive regime. "The progress of mankind onward and upward forever" said little to someone whose home, family and future had been destroyed by some arbitrary governmental decisions based on racial classifications. Sacrifice and suffering were what we needed to talk about, and the nature and reality of evil.

In retrospect, I see what a painful period this was for the members of Cape Town's Unitarian church, and I suspect that I, as an American humanist, was not really the best person to help them through this time. They had their hands full coping with the nation's enormous race problems that resulted from apartheid. Ultimately I don't think the congregation was really ready to accept American-style Unitarianism. Nominally, they were liberal just like we are liberal, but their form of liberalism was political and social, whereas mine was more theological. Still, I did the best I could as their minister throughout the duration of my initial three-year contract with the church in Cape Town, and after three years they offered me a contract extension.

But Trudi and I believed it was probably time to return to the U.S. We hadn't gone home at all during those three years, and Trudi worried about her mother becoming ill. We had discussed the fact that if something happened back home, we could probably afford for Trudi to fly back to the States but not return again to Cape Town, and there hadn't been any conversation with the church leadership about whether they would help with travel expenses in that situation.

Our concerns about Trudi's mother were our main reason for not staying longer in South Africa, but the fact that our children were approaching school age was an issue as well. In Cape Town, the white children were placed in a system called National Christian education. There was a school near our house, and occasionally the school band would march past. It struck me that they looked like Hitler youth, dressed in their brown uniforms and marching in formation. That really made me uneasy.

Another time, Nancie and Trudi and I boarded a city bus that had a line in the middle saying whites should sit ahead of the line and nonwhites behind, although the driver himself was coloured. There was a black woman in the back, and for some reason Nancie ran down the aisle and scrambled into her lap. Trudi hurried back to fetch her and the woman said it was fine, but I didn't want to raise our children somewhere where we'd have to explain bus segregation. So after three years, we started preparing to return to the U.S.

~11~

1972-1977: North Adams

I informed the UUA of my decision to leave, but I was too far away to do any candidating and find a new position. So we flew from Cape Town back to Auburn, New York, and stayed with Trudi's family for a few months while I looked for my next ministerial posting.

The UUA sent me to candidate at a church in North Adams, Massachusetts. The process for candidating is that you submit letters and sermons, and if the search committee likes what it sees you're invited to preach at a so-called neutral pulpit, which is someplace other than the actual church that is looking to hire where their search committee can see you in action. The next step after that is to be invited to the church to do services on two consecutive Sundays. In the week between the two Sundays, you meet with church committees and small groups of congregants.

After going through that process in North Adams, I was offered the position. Theirs was a small congregation in a big building. It was common in the late 1800s for Universalist churches to believe that great growth lay in their future, so they built churches much larger than they currently needed, preparing for a hundred years later. One church historian pointed out that these buildings were designed to hold conventions. The Universalists held a large convention every year, and each congregation wanted to be chosen to host, but of course the reality was that each church would be used for that only once every thirty years or so. So we ended up with churches designed to hold over one hundred people for services usually attended by thirty or forty.

Another significant thing about the North Adams church was that this was the beginning of serious attempts in the U.S., or at least in New England, by social services organizations to mitigate the growing problem of drug addiction. An organization called Emergency Trips made up of local volunteers was renting the church building for that purpose. But it was overwhelming. Their mission was to get kids who were using drugs off the streets and offer them treatment. But the organization didn't have any money or trained staff, so what they considered counselors were really just young volunteers with no idea of what they were doing. Honestly I would not be surprised if they made the drug problem worse, not better.

And they didn't know the simplest things about running an organization, like they'd have meetings and forget to lock up after themselves when they were done, and things would be stolen from the office. When the program fell apart and no longer paid rent, the church never really got back on its feet. There was a Head Start preschool renting the building as well, but there was just never enough revenue coming in.

We were spending down the church's savings just to maintain the building, which needed a lot of work. One day we noticed that the ground floor was beginning to warp. A contractor came to look at it and discovered that the floor consisted of beams that had been laid directly on a layer of sand. Fixing that would cost thousands of dollars. A roofing company had told the church officials prior to my arrival that the slate roof would need to be replaced. But when I had someone else come out to look at where it was leaking, he said that there was no reason to replace the roof, and that the roofing company knew that they would make thousands of dollars reselling the slate if they did it. Instead, for a fee of two hundred dollars he climbed up with a bucket of tar and plugged the holes. It was sobering to see that even when dealing with a church, people can be such crooks.

Our family moved into the parsonage, which was not on church grounds but was within walking distance, a large old Victorian house with a walk-up attic. It was a beautiful home to live in although I was glad the church paid our heating bill, since it was large and drafty and not very well insulated! We enrolled Nathan and Nancie in the school run by the teacher training program at nearby North Adams State College.

The church closed for the summer, so we were able to spend all of July and August at our cottage in Vermont, which was wonderful for all of us. We'd walk in the woods, attend summer-stock theater productions, go to movies, browse bookstores and antique shops. Trudi and I had a tradition of searching out all of the area's ice cream stands. There was a pond where the kids could swim. Our neighbors down the road were Alan Seaburg and his wife Jean. They had two daughters who were a few years older than our children, and one of them, Carolyn, wanted to be a teacher, so she ran a summer school where our children colored and learned their letters and numbers.

Alan's brother Carl Seaburg, a writer and theologian who wrote several of the hymns in the Unitarian Universalist hymnal, lived in a cabin on the same property, and the two brothers had a vision that they were going to make the woods of Vermont their permanent home. They planned to make a living writing and maybe start a college, for which the students who enrolled would help build the buildings they needed.

It was a good, UU-like fantasy, but it came to a hasty end the very first year that they tried to stay past summer. In November, Carl decided his cabin was too cold. Alan and Jean had put a furnace in the main house and thought they could manage it, but one day Jean said to Alan, "I don't mind starving and I don't mind if you starve, but if we don't earn some money the girls are going to starve, and that I *do* mind." And so they packed up the car and drove back to their year-round home in Medford, Massachusetts, where Alan was soon hired as a curator of manuscripts at Harvard Divinity School, and Jean found work at a library. Carl's great American novel would just have to wait.

My tenure at the North Adams church lasted for five years, from 1972 to 1977. But in light of the church's failing finances, the congregation voted to downsize by purchasing a smaller building on the North Adams-Williamstown town line in hopes of attracting congregants from both towns, and it was once again time for me to find a new ministerial home.

~12~

1977-2001: Carlisle

When I was in theological school, we would occasionally ruminate about what the ideal church would look like. One of my colleagues said that the ideal UU church would be in a rural community twenty-five miles from downtown Boston. Well, strangely enough, that's just what we found at that point: the First Religious Society in Carlisle. I went through the candidating process once again and received the job, and in January 1977, Trudi, the children and I moved into the parsonage, a small Cape located directly next door to the church and across the street from Carlisle's K-8 public school.

We were happy in Carlisle right away. The small congregation contained many families similar to ours, with school-aged children, and we all made a lot of friends. Trudi joined the bridge club. We were close enough to Boston and Cambridge that I could be at Harvard University in a half-hour for my regular UUA Historical Board meetings. Though there were no retail shops in

Carlisle itself, we were an easy drive to neighboring towns that had all kinds of shops. The kids liked their new school. It turned out to be a perfect match for us, and I remained at the Carlisle church until my retirement in 2001.

Our first few years in Carlisle, it was really a struggle to keep the church running financially. The treasurer, Irene Miller, would occasionally pay the oil bill out of her own checking account, and then when there was enough money in the church account she'd pay herself back. Well, appointing a treasurer wealthy enough to pay the bills herself is not really a very sound business plan! Fortunately, we received rent from The Red Balloon, a cooperative preschool located in the church basement.

We had a terrific staff who helped the church get through those lean years while we paid them very little: our organist, our choir director, our groundskeeper. And the congregation was so supportive and committed to the church's success. We were still a small church, but the loyalty of the parishioners and the fact that people were willing to work so hard made up for our size. We had groups that met in the parsonage to discuss books and religion. We had a volunteer-led religious education program. The church ran an annual antique fair during the years that antiques were really popular; we had our yearly

Strawberry Festival in June, the Harvest Fair in October, the Greens Sale in December. Each endeavor was a huge volunteer effort that raised money for the church, brought our members together working hard and purposefully, and drew townspeople and neighbors into our community.

About two years into my tenure at the First Religious Society, the church leadership decided we needed a stronger program for our teens. We came up with the idea of hiring a student from theological school to lead them, and we soon find an ideal candidate, Eric Heller, who was a Vietnam vet. He and his wife worked with our high school students, leading discussion groups, organizing field trips into Boston, hosting sleepovers. Eric stayed in that role for two years, and because his work with the teens was so successful, we continued the teen ministry program with other theological students. They brought a whole new point of view and a new approach to our church. People of all ages responded well to them, and that program really became one of FRS's greatest assets.

The only condition attached to hiring a student minister, according to the UUA, was that I would be required to take classes at one of the regional theological schools to make me an effective supervisor. I considered Harvard and Boston University, then drove out to Andover

Newton Theological School, which distinguished itself merely by the fact that it was a fast, easy commute on Route 128 and had a large amount of free parking, unlike Cambridge or Boston.

But beyond that initial advantage, I found that it was an excellent choice for me. The faculty was terrific and I liked the class I was required to take on how to supervise students. And then the dean mentioned that as settled ministers, we students could enroll in their doctor of ministry program for a very low tuition. So I talked it over with Trudi and decided to do it.

Grateful for the unexpected opportunity to study at Andover Newton, I took as many courses as I could on spiritual development and eventually wrote my doctoral dissertation on that topic. The students at Andover Newton were a diverse mix of Unitarian Universalists, Greek Orthodox, Congregationalists, Catholics, Church of the Nazarene, Baptists, and others. We had a wonderful teacher, a Catholic nun called Sister Letitia who also taught priests in training at Boston College Theological School. The first day of class, she said to us, "I will not tolerate arguing about personal theology. God saves whomever God chooses in whatever way God wishes, and if you want to argue with each other, don't do it in my classroom."

Spiritual development is a topic I've struggled with for years. A major breakthrough in my thinking came when I read something about George Santayana, a Spanish Roman Catholic philosopher who taught at Harvard. He attended Mass every morning and spent his days writing books on naturalism, which is what we would now call atheism. One day a student said to him, "Dr. Santayana, you write books on naturalism and you go to Mass every morning. How do you explain that contradiction?"

His inscrutable reply was, "There is no God, and Mary is His mother."

And really, that paradoxical statement from George Santayana perfectly sums up my beliefs as well. When I started theological school, Unitarians and Universalists alike, still unmerged, were passionately discussing humanism in the sense of a form of agnosticism or atheism that is still religious. I consider myself that kind of humanist. What I mean by that is that I believe in a set of spiritual values which we keep separate from our secular values, and we can use those values to make meaning of our lives. We UU humanists are religious people of faith, and I am happy with that, even if it manifests in effect as "There is no God and Jesus is his son." It doesn't make sense. It's a paradox. But life is paradoxical.

The small town of Carlisle changed significantly during our years there. Trudi commented one day that when we first arrived, all the cars parked in front of the church were small American cars, Pintos and Vegas, but that she had just seen a Volvo. Well, this was a small detail, but it was true that the town was becoming more upscale. Carlisle has two-acre and four-acre zoning, and many of the house lots were even larger than that, which was a very appealing feature to wealthy home-buyers. Throughout the 1980s, the population grew both in number and in income level.

This had a positive ripple effect on us. Church growth depends largely on having a changing population. Once people get settled in a particular church or in the habit of not going to church at all, it's very difficult to get them to change their ways. So having a town with a growing population meant new people were moving in who were looking for a place to worship and to find a sense of community. We had one family who had attended the Congregational church in town before they came to us. A short time after they began attending, they said to me, "At the other church, no one would talk to us. Here people seemed eager right away to get to know us."

We were definitely doing some things right as a church. But of course, dealing with more difficult matters is part of a minister's job as well. A commonly cited statistic among people who study churches says that after you've attended a church for about six months, you begin unconsciously internalizing the idea that the way things are done is the way they should be done and there's no reason for change. That has always happened to some degree at FRS just as at every church.

And inevitably, ministers have to help congregations through really tumultuous life events such as divorces and death. When it came to challenging pastoral matters, I relied heavily on the faculty at Andover Newton for guidance, especially my faculty supervisor, Jerry Handspicker. Memorial services were often difficult, though in a small congregation, that wasn't a frequent thing and often involved elderly people.

But there were exceptions. One was when an eighteen-year-old in our congregation died over Thanksgiving weekend in a car accident. That was awful. And it was another one of those times when having Trudi by my side was the greatest pastoral support. She was so good with people, and we both understood that all we could do was be there with the family, sit with the family. We couldn't say anything to make it better. I remember at the funeral, family members tossed coins into the gravesite.

This was something new to me, but apparently it's a Russian Orthodox tradition, and that was part of the young man's mother's heritage.

One of the most identifiable challenges for FRS during my tenure there was a secrecy about money. Pledging and fundraising are often problematic at any church, but all the more so when it's the parish's tradition to keep monetary issues shrouded in secrecy. Trudi liked to say that people would rather talk about their sex lives than money. The UU church in Concord printed a list of annual pledges: not giving names of who had pledged, just amounts. I tried that in our newsletter one time and was severely chastised by several parishioners who were scandalized by what they considered a revealing of confidential information. Even without attaching names to it!

In 1994, we built onto the church for the first time in many decades. We needed more office space for staff, better accessibility, a safer fire escape, larger restrooms and a modern kitchen. For years, the church kitchen had been located in the basement. Since coffee hour and just about all of our social events happened in Union Hall, on the ground floor, that meant endless effort had to be expended carrying food and dishes upstairs and downstairs!

Getting the addition built seemed to be twice as much work as it should have, because we came up with a budget, took bids and selected an architect. Then when it came time to take a congregational vote on allotting the money, the architect surprised us all by saying there would be an additional $100,000 in architect fees beyond the number we thought we'd agreed upon for the project. This was impossible for us, so we had to start all over again. But finally, a different architect got the job done for us.

When we had time off, we'd go to New York to see family. Trudi's family had a large reunion every August which I still attend. We'd go to Vermont every summer, staying with the Seaburgs after we sold our cabin. We sometimes went to see our nephew in Brattleboro as well. Occasionally Trudi's family would visit us in Carlisle; my siblings never did.

The kids attended the Carlisle Public School, right across the street from the parsonage, through eighth grade, then went to Concord-Carlisle High School. Trudi took a job at a local company called Assurance Technology, where she worked in bookkeeping and payroll along with handling the boss's mail. Trudi was always such a whiz-bang with numbers and accounting. She could look at an entire page of figures and say, "Something is off here."

Then she'd sit down and find out what it was. All employees at Assurance Technology worked for hourly pay rather than on salary, so there were a lot of time sheets to keep track of, and Trudi could figure out immediately when someone wasn't keeping their hours correctly. She even required the boss to turn in a time sheet!

When work was especially busy for her, she'd ask me to come keep her company at the office while she stayed until eleven or twelve at night. It was just a five-minute drive from the parsonage, so I'd go join her in the late evening, and while she was in her office doing her work, I'd sit down at one of the secretaries' desks and write my sermons. She'd be ready to go home at midnight or one in the morning and she'd still get up at five o'clock to clean the house, do the laundry and get to work on time.

Despite her many capabilities, Trudi suffered from bouts of severe depression, and there were times when she wasn't able to function well at home or at work. We spent a lot of time in therapy learning how to manage her depression together. It was all worthwhile, though. She brought so much to my life. She was so effective at pastoral care, especially sitting with people who were ill. She'd sit up all night with someone who was in the end stages of life, just keeping them company with silent compassion in a way that is so difficult to do. When she wasn't depressed, she had boundless energy, which is certainly not something I have ever possessed. She had a funny habit of arriving at church late on Sunday mornings even though we lived right next door. From the pulpit as I was beginning my sermon, I'd see her slip in fifteen minutes late. Everyone else would see her as well, and smile at her habitual tardiness.

We returned several times to England in those years. We always loved spending time in London, and took trips from there to Scotland and Wales as well. We'd rent a car and drive around the countryside, staying in bed-and-breakfasts. One summer we went on a walking tour in Yorkshire with Carlisle friends. We stayed at a little hotel and took long walks in the countryside every day. One particularly memorable walk on that trip took us through an abandoned mansion. The builders had unwittingly sited it on top of an ancient Roman tin mine. The mine's tunnel collapsed and the whole stone mansion broke in half. That was a really interesting sight. Another time we visited Beatrix Potter's hillside cottage. And we always returned on those trips to Tavistock Square in London to visit the Gandhi statue we'd first discovered when we were en route to Cape Town.

~13~

2001-Present: Retirement

I retired from the First Religious Society – and was subsequently named Minister Emeritus – when the church year ended in June of 2001. I was sixty-eight, and although there was no traditional retirement age for ministers, Trudi felt it was time. The previous year we'd purchased a house in Billerica and moved out of the parsonage. It seemed like an affordable way to stay near Carlisle and FRS. Our daughter Nancie was living with us at that time and Nathan lived in Acton.

I had mixed feelings about retiring. On the one hand, I felt that I could happily continue as minister forever; on the other hand I don't think that's the healthiest thing for any church. And now I can look back and see that a change in ministers was a very positive move for FRS. The church has significantly developed and changed and grown since my retirement, and I'm tremendously pleased about that.

The biggest issue we faced in terms of potential conflict within the church was making a decision about becoming a Welcoming Congregation, meaning we proactively reached out to, welcomed and incorporated the LGBT community. We eventually make that decision, but not without a fair amount of debate and conflicting opinions. The other question we struggled with for a while involved how to invest a couple of large bequests we received, but that was resolved in time as well.

I myself was in favor of the Welcoming Congregation designation. My belief is that people fall in love with people because of who they are, not necessarily because of their gender. I've seen many same-sex couples enjoy long-term relationships and happy marriages. Some of them didn't even consider themselves gay or lesbian; it was just a matter of falling in love with a certain person when that person came along.

And of course, it's fun for a minister to perform weddings of any kind. The Unitarian Universalist faith is flexible when it comes to the wedding ceremony; it can be standard or the couple can write the whole thing themselves. I enjoy seeing what people come up with for their wedding. It's interesting to learn what they believe is important about their relationship and what kind of oath they want to take. Not all marriages last, but I understand that as well. People sometimes grow in different directions.

We made a few more trips to England after I retired, but Trudi was developing dementia, and eventually she reached the point where it didn't feel safe for her to travel. Her memory was fading too fast. After that, a lot of my time went into caring for her. I served as part-time interim minister in Billerica for two years and continue to preach there as a regular guest minister, which I'm happy to be able to do. I've always liked preaching. I spend a lot of my time in retirement reading as well: theology, poetry, World War II history. I've joined a couple of poetry discussion groups and written some poetry of my own as well. In 2010, with the help of Alex and Linda Beavers, two former parishioners who are in the publishing business, I published *Life Wins,* a collection of my sermons which is now listed on Amazon.

In January of 1997, while our daughter Nancie and her husband were living in Waltham, their daughter Stefanie was born. From her earliest days, she was a huge part of our life. When she was still very young, her parents separated, and Nancie and Stefanie moved in with us. The house we bought in Billerica had an in-law apartment which was perfect for the two of them. And having them so close by meant that we had the joy of watching her grow up every step of the way. Until Stefanie was old enough to go to school, Trudi babysat for her while Nancie was at work. Stefanie and I had a game we called "Three Little Pigs," in which her imaginary house was the space under my desk. Stefanie's companionship has been a constant source of joy in my life from the time she was born right up through the present day.

Trudi remained active and sociable until shortly after we moved to Billerica, when her dementia was overtaking her mind. The dementia manifested then in some strange behaviors. She filled in crossword puzzles with random letters and cut the corners of post cards. Later, I heard about some neurological research that suggested behavior like this was the brain's attempt to hold on to some semblance of organizing function.

In 2013 she became suddenly ill. We thought she had pneumonia, but at the hospital she was diagnosed with ovarian cancer, and we were told she was too weak to withstand treatment. Instead, she was set up with hospice care at home, but she faded away very quickly after that. It is a relief to know she didn't suffer for long.

Seeing Stefanie develop her identity as an adult is an ongoing source of delight for me. Throughout her years of college, she has become increasingly involved in social action, justice, and Latinx and gay pride. She takes every opportunity she can find to travel, and has already visited many parts of Europe and other places. She graduated from college in May of 2019 and is planning on a career applying psychology to the academic world. She's a wonderful person and a legacy in which I take tremendous pride. And she never stops taking care of me.

When Trudi died, we had a beautiful service for her at FRS, and I know the same will be true for me someday. Her body was cremated, as mine will be, and once I am gone our ashes will be scattered together. Even now, when I think about Trudi, I marveled at the ways in which she changed my life. Spending nine years of my childhood in hospitals meant that I was never really socialized in a typical way. As a result, I've never been very good at interpersonal stuff. But Trudi made up for that. She was always good with people. That helped me personally and also professionally; I truly believe that I was hired for some of my ministerial roles because of how she presented herself as my spouse and my more social half.

I take comfort in the idea that once our ashes are scattered in the Memorial Garden, we will be together there for a very long time. Or maybe the ashes will disappear from the Memorial Garden with the first rainstorm, but

Trudi and I will be together again for a very long time nonetheless.

I am an intellectual agnostic, some days an atheist, and an emotional theist verging on Christian, if that makes any sense. I find most God talk offensive. God is a hard concept for me to grasp with my mind but an easy one to love with my heart. Touches of mysticism certainly help the heart bit. I love reading some of the cosmology material – string theory and the concept that everything was created out of nothing and that maybe all of the pluses and minuses in the universe add up to zero. I don't understand it, and the math is far beyond my meager algebra and geometry, but I find it like listening to a great piece of music – "The Triumphal March" from *Aida* says something if I could just understand the words....

More and more I believe in Universalism: "Go forth and preach the Gospel, the good news, to all creation." I am fond of the early Christian scholar Origen of Alexandria. I believe he was on to something when he decided that freedom of choice, free will, was the tragedy and the potential source of salvation for all sentient beings. Choice is more possible than we often realize, and one of the functions of the church is to open up the possibilities of life to people.

I also like Origen because of his concept of interrelatedness and the universality of the love of God. He was a good ecologist. His mythology may not fit our times, but his vision does. As some ancient Greek said, "A myth is a false account bearing truth."

Therapy helped me realize that sometimes our lives are the way they are because of our own perceptions, and that those perceptions are changeable. The analogy is that of a map. Maps show what we are interested in or think important, and sometimes we leave out a lot or include stuff we don't need to include. Religion can be lessons in redrawing our maps.

Professor Jerry Handspicker at Andover Newton taught Neuro-Linguistic Programming as well as communications and theology. NLP is weird and gimmicky, but I was enamored of it because it works and it provides valuable insights, such as the fact that your life map is yours and you can redraw it anytime you want to. I don't think any gimmicky stuff is necessarily a substitute for real therapy, but it does work – I was cured of a spider phobia of 45 years' duration in a matter of minutes and the cure still holds. Sometimes it helps us to have permission to change, and the church can give us that permission in many ways, even with gimmicks.

I love the constant suggestion in ministry that we ought to be growing. We cannot acquire too many skills, learn too much, think too much, stretch our minds too much. I love the fact that I am paid to do those things. I love solitude. I spent a great deal of my childhood alone, and in solitude I find great comfort and strength. Sometimes I get downright antisocial and I go off by myself to recharge my soul. As Trudi pointed out, that is not always a useful habit for a minister.

Ministers are shamans, magicians, witches and warlocks. Our job is who we are as well as what we do, and, as someone said at a conference some years, ago we can't ever take that extra drink, tell that dirty story, without violating what we are supposed to be. Or, we might add, violate a trust, break confidentiality, abuse our positions, corrupt our relationships with people, believe that it does not matter what we do. Who we are is important to people, and if we want to be ministers, important to us. What we deal in is spells and magic as well as facts and knowledge. Ministers deal with possibilities and ideals and dreams and hopes and people's hearts. We are not good magicians if we break those hearts.

Magic is an art rather than a science. I think of ministry and religion as being about art – poetry. John

Haynes Holmes in 1935 wrote in *The Beacon Song and Service Book*, "When I say 'God' it is poetry and not theology." I suspect the universe of being more a poem than a collection of facts.

Earlier I described my first full-blown mystical experience, which happened while I was studying at Tufts. In the many years since then, similar experiences have occurred on a few occasions. I stepped out of the front door of the church in Carlisle once, and there came to me the phrase "underneath are the everlasting arms." I had the certainty that I was looking through the physical world before me at reality, and that indeed I could see the reality of the phrase. (In all candor, I ought to report that a very real image of Jesus holding out his arms in blessing is associated with that memory, but I had the sense that I was trying to put a recognizable image to something incomprehensible.)

Another time I left my physician's office after a frustrating discussion of health problems, and in the middle of the parking lot I was hit by the same type of sensation, only this time the message was that I was going to die: not necessarily right away or even soon, but eventually. It struck me then as one of the most liberating things I could know. I sat in my car for what seemed a long time, too overwhelmed to drive – taken with the wonder and beauty of it all.

For a full week, I felt buoyed by the thought of how free the knowledge of our mortality makes us, not in an intellectual but an emotional sense – death, I remember thinking at the time, is a gift. "Nothing lasts forever" was the phrase that came to me, and it was a happy thought. Those experiences continue to happen now and again, though usually not as spectacular.

In retrospect, I do not regret as much as I once thought I did. The map of my life journey is *my* map, and I have learned to redraw it, repair it, find things on it I had forgotten, and downscale things I used to draw large. I keep working on that map.

~14~

Summing Up

I have two favourite quotations that I rely on. The first is the George Santayana quotation I referred to earlier: "There is no God and Mary is His Mother." The other is from Wallace Stevens: "The final belief is to believe in a fiction, which you know to be a fiction, there being nothing else. The exquisite truth is to know that it is a fiction and that you believe it willingly." And a recent addition to my canon, an exquisite poem by Tess Gallagher titled "Opening": "I entered this world not wanting / to come. I'll leave it not / wanting to go. All this while, / when it seemed there were two doors, / there was only one – this / passing through."

Back in the 1960s, folk-song style music was big, and Leonard Cohen had one called "Passing Through," with the repeated lines, "Passing through, passing through / Sometimes happy, sometimes blue / Glad that I ran into you / Tell the people that you saw me passing through."

The Universe is, we guess, 13.75 billion years old, give or take a few billion. And perhaps stranger than we think, it is even suggested that all of this is a hologram projected from a black hole. Goodness! I knew a Unitarian Universalist minister who preached a sermon on "Bits of Nothing" which seems to be what we might be made up of. On the other hand, I am agnostic enough to appreciate that some years ago, a faculty member of a Mennonite college asked the question, "Why may not a creator God create a creative creation?"

What I lost, missed, in my growing up, because of (or not?) the Tb and the hospital experience, was a religious community. I am grateful that, working in Cortland, New York, I found the Universalist church and Trudi was a member. For me church offers a community based on love, respect, sharing life. I suspect capitalism of being the religion or pseudo-religion of our culture: it has all the features of a religion, the saved and the damned, rituals, places of worship. Or any of the other "isms" which have troubled our human journey. But religious communities can offer us better alternatives: Love one another, be kind to living things, all the other wonderful and sometimes weird ways of walking gently on the earth. Hearkening back once again to Origen, considered one of the "Fathers" of the

Christian church, we find the belief that all sentient beings had immortal souls. A weird and wonderful fiction, perhaps, but calling on us to respect and love all living things.

The Muslim Emperor of India Akbar the Great (1542-1605) had a Mosque built with this inscription on the entry gate: "Jesus, Son of Mary (on whom be peace) said: The World is a Bridge, pass over it, but build no houses upon it. He who hopes for a day, may hope for eternity; but the World endures but an hour. Spend it in prayer, for the rest is unseen."

Meister Eckhart (1260-1328) left us this: "If the only prayer you ever say is Thank You, it will be enough."

Thank You.

ABOUT THE EDITOR

Nancy Shohet West is a Boston-area journalist who helps individuals, multi-generational families, communities, and special interest groups to write and self-publish their memoirs. For more information, go to www.NancyShohetWest.com.

Made in the USA
Middletown, DE
18 September 2019